lonely planet

ANTARCTICA

Alexis Averbuck, Liz Carlson

Meet Our Writers

Alexis Averbuck

alexisaverbuck.com

Alexis lived in Antarctica for a life-changing year in her 20s. The raw landscape, extreme remoteness and spectacular visual and emotional experiences turned her into a painter. Though she writes with words here, sometimes they aren't enough for a place like Antarctica. She now lives on a Greek island, but Antarctica keeps calling her back home.

Liz Carlson

@youngadventuress

Liz Carlson is a travel writer, photographer and polar expedition guide in the Arctic and Antarctic. She has spent years working in remote regions, both guiding and documenting expeditions, with a focus on polar history, landscapes and the realities of travel at the ends of the Earth.

LIZ CARLSON

PREVIOUS SPREAD: VADIM_N/SHUTTERSTOCK

Above Juvenile Antarctic fur seal, Prion Island (p87), South Georgia

Contents

OVERSNAP/GETTY IMAGES

Above Southern right whale, Paradise Harbor (p107), Antarctic Peninsula

ESSAYS

VISUAL GUIDES

HOW HIGH?

Average elevation: 2250m (including the floating ice shelves)/2194m (excluding the ice shelves)

Highest point: Vinson Massif (4897m)

Highest point of Antarctic Plateau: Dome A (4093m)

Highest mountain on Antarctic Peninsula: Mt Jackson (3184m)

AWE-INSPIRING **LANDSCAPE**

Antarctica possesses an unnamable quality. Call it inspiration, call it grandeur…it is simply the indescribable feeling of being a small speck in an austere, vast and beautiful land. A domain where striated ice towers float among geometric pancake ice, literally untouched mountains rear from marine mist, and wildlife lives, year in and year out, to its own rhythms, quite apart from human concerns.

Left Volcanic steam cave, Mt Erebus (p147), Ross Sea **Right** The Andes (p44), Parque Nacional Tierra del Fuego **Below** Deception Island volcano harbor (p100), Antarctic Peninsula

→ FLY OVER THE ANDES

Overflights are the caviar of travel, whether in Antarctica proper or from Ushuaia up through the peaks of the Andes (p44).

SILMCX/SHUTTERSTOCK

SET DOWN THAT CAMERA

Yes, yes, incredible shots. Get them (p164)! Then set down the gear and just soak it all in.

FROM LEFT: CAVAN IMAGES/ALAMY; VITALII PANOK/SHUTTERSTOCK

↑ VOLCANIC LANDS

Feel the power of the piping peak of the Ross Sea's Mt Erebus (p146) and ash-covered snow and geothermal waters inside Deception Island's volcano harbor (p100).

Best Scenic Experiences

- **Photograph dramatic cliffs and sparkling bergs in Lemaire Channel.** (p107)
- **Round the Peninsula to find Hope Bay's tabular icebergs and Brown Bluff's volcanic cliffs.** (p125)
- **Stay at futuristic Echo Base, perched on a glacier.** (p183)
- **Track Shackleton, Amundsen and Scott's paths to the Pole.** (p206)
- **Spend the night under the stars at an *estancia* in Tierra del Fuego.** (p58)

AMAZING ACROBATS

Emperor penguins capture prey by pursuit-diving to amazing depths and durations: up to 535m and 22 minutes.

The blue whale is the largest animal on Earth, reaching 200 tonnes and 33.5m.

Elephant seals have huge reservoirs of blood (22% of their body mass) which helps them dive to 1930m.

WILDLIFE **ENCOUNTERS**

Antarctica is preserved by the Antarctic Treaty, and some of the world's most extraordinary species flourish here. Some, such as the enormous whales, migrate from afar, while others, including the Weddell seal and emperor penguin, remain close to the continent. Millions of seabirds skim the Southern Ocean. Wildlife is generally unafraid of humans: visitors usually elicit no more than an uninterested yawn from seals and penguins focused on their young.

Left Juvenile Weddell seal (p122)
Right Adélie penguins (p120), Paulet Island (p125), Antarctic Peninsula
Below Macaroni penguin eggs (p121)

→ SAFE DISTANCES

When viewing wildlife, keep your distance. The Guidelines for Visitors to the Antarctic require it – and it's important for animal and human safety alike.

Scan here for the full guidelines.

ANDREW PEACOCK/GETTY IMAGES

BIRDWATCHING UNDERWAY

Remember to go out on deck while your ship is sailing to spot albatross, petrels, cormorants and other seabirds (p141) circling the Southern Ocean.

FROM LEFT: GOINYK PRODUCTION/SHUTTERSTOCK, BUTTERFLY VOYAGES · SERGE OUACHEE/WIKIMEDIA, CC-BY-SA 3.0

↑ MACARONI EGGS

Macaroni penguins lay two eggs. The smaller first-laid egg (left) is usually kicked out of the nest soon after the larger egg (right) is laid and only one hatches.

Best Wildlife Experiences

- **Spy elephant seals noisily alongside nesting penguins at South Georgia Island.** (p84)
- **Revel in rarefied wildlife viewing at emperor penguin rookeries.** (p131)
- **See huge fin whale pods along the Peninsula and the South Orkney Islands.** (p123)
- **Find fur seal colonies on subantarctic islands, and lone leopard seals in the ice.** (p122)
- **Enter a birder's paradise on New Zealand's subantarctic islands.** (p172)

ADVENTURE ACTIVITIES

Antarctica's surreal remoteness, extreme cold, enormous ice shelves and mountain ranges, and exotic life forms challenge you to embrace life and its trials. Ice and weather, not clocks and calendars, determine itineraries and timetables for all expeditions here. You can climb Antarctic peaks or kayak icy waters. And there's nothing quite like strapping on the crampons to ascend magnificent glaciers or skiing the sheer expanse of the polar ice cap.

Left Antarctic Ice Marathon (p187), Union Glacier **Right** Kayaking, Neko Harbor (p107), Antarctic Peninsula **Below** Scuba diving, Antarctic Peninsula (p92)

→ KAYAK BETWEEN ICEBERGS

Imagine your blades cutting the clear surface as you glide between towering icebergs and brilliantly hued ice, seals zipping through the water beneath. Book it!

JAY DICKMAN/GETTY IMAGES

CAMPOUT, ANTARCTIC STYLE

Some cruises offer overnight tent camping on the land, out under the jam-packed stars in the austral sky.

FROM LEFT: MIKE KING/LNP/SHUTTERSTOCK, BIOSPHOTO/ALAMY

↑ SCUBA DIVING

Expert scuba divers head into the mysterious depths around Ushuaia (p41), but also in Antarctica – check your cruise offerings (p219).

Best Adventure Experiences

- **Undertake an epic climb of Vinson Massif, Antarctica's highest point.** (p131)
- **Fly, or cross-country ski to the South Pole.** (p130)
- **If a warm soak in volcanic waters at Deception Island is too tame for you, take a polar plunge.** (p161)
- **Run a marathon at Union Glacier or Schirmacher Oasis.** (p187)
- **Hike under ice-topped mountains at Parque Nacional Tierra del Fuego.** (p42)

WINDS OF TIME

Katabatic winds, like Douglas Mawson endured, are caused by denser, colder air rushing down off the polar plateau to the coast.

Katabatics achieve velocities of up to 320km/h.

A time capsule of 1950s Antarctic life still exists at Detaille Island.

TRACE THE STEPS **OF EXPLORERS**

The names of renowned explorers and their sovereigns, benefactors and families are superimposed on Antarctica's shores. They tried to penetrate this vast, mysterious land, with varying degrees of success. Visitors follow in their footsteps and imagine what it was like to forge through pack ice on a creaking wooden boat or haul sledges across the polar plateau. Historic huts even remain, frozen in rime ice, telling the story of adventures long past.

Left Katabatic winds, Ross Sea (p134) **Right** Tinned food, Shackleton's Hut (p144), Cape Royds **Below** Museo Marítimo & Museo del Presidio (p47), Ushuaia

→ DINNER AT SHACKLETON'S PLACE

At Ernest Shackleton's *Nimrod* expedition hut (p144), tins of food with unappetizing names (boiled mutton, lunch tongue, pea powder) await diners who will never return.

CHRIS WALKER/CHICAGO TRIBUNE/
TRIBUNE NEWS SERVICE VIA GETTY IMAGES

WINDBLOWN LIFE AT CAPE DENISON

To learn more about Douglas Mawson's 1911 stay at Commonwealth Bay, pounded by gravity-driven winds called katabatics, read his book *Home of the Blizzard*.

FROM LEFT: ARTHUR GREENBERG/ALAMY; SERGI REBOREDO/VW PICS/UNIVERSAL

↑ MUSEUM PREPARATION

Ushuaia's museums (p46) and the Historic Dockyard Museum (p71) in Stanley set the stage of the early days of exploration – great preparation for your trip further south.

Best Historical Experiences

- **Ogle the perfectly preserved Antarctic exploration relics in Shackleton's hut.** (p144)
- **Visit Scott's eerily intact *Terra Nova* hut.** (p145)
- **Walk through history at South Georgia's Grytviken whaling station.** (p76)
- **Adventure to Borchgrevink's huts, Antarctica's oldest buildings and home to the first overwintering group.** (p143)
- **Visit the house that became Nordenskjöld's unplanned home for two years.** (p127)

RESEARCH SUPPORT & OVERSIGHT

The Council of Managers of National Antarctic Programs (COMNAP; comnap.aq) offers a full list of bases and programs, plus an interactive map.

The Scientific Committee on Antarctic Research (SCAR; scar.org) oversees the science.

SCIENCE ON ICE

Since its earliest exploration, Antarctica has been a land of discovery. Many of the initial expeditions were undertaken to learn whether the fabled Terra Australis Incognita (p161) existed, and then, once it had been identified, to determine its extent, properties, flora and fauna. In the modern era, with the creation of the Antarctic Treaty, Antarctica became the one protected continent in the world, reserved almost exclusively for scientific research.

Left Mario Zucchelli Station (p168), Terra Nova Bay, Ross Sea **Right** Neutrino detector, South Pole (p178) **Below** Türkiye's 9th National Antarctic Science Expedition

→ SOUTH POLE OBSERVATIONS

The South Pole is topped by a high-tech station surrounded by cutting-edge astrophysical observation equipment (including a neutrino detector array buried 1.9km below the ice).

CARLO BOLLO/ALAMY

HOMO SAPIENS

It's not just animals that scientists study. Research on humans stationed in Antarctica include studying the effects of winter isolation, diet and exercise, and seasonal changes in climate and UV light.

FROM LEFT: ANDREW PEACOCK/GETTY IMAGES, SEBNEM COSKUN/ANADOLU VIA GETTY IMAGES

↑ ANTARCTIC TREATY

Under the treaty (p192), Antarctica is a continent reserved for science. Disciplines include biochemistry, physiology, genomics, seismology, physics, astronomy and climate (p168).

Best Science Experiences

- **Tour McMurdo Station or Scott Base in the Ross Sea region.** (p168)
- **See where sophisticated measurements from outer space are observed at the South Pole.** (p191)
- **Visit one of more than 10 stations packed on small King George Island.** (p97)
- **Help track birds and whales from Antarctica and around the world with eBird and Happywhale.** (p168)

ISLAND LIFE

The subantarctic islands, circling the continent, are as exotic a destination as Antarctica itself. Many are rarely visited, and all make for warmer-weather, protected homes for wildlife. Some, like the Falkland Islands (Islas Malvinas), are inhabited and with a culture all their own. On the Eastern side of the continent, you can follow in the footsteps of Māori who first discovered the Auckland Islands, or watch plumes above Mt Erebus on Ross Island.

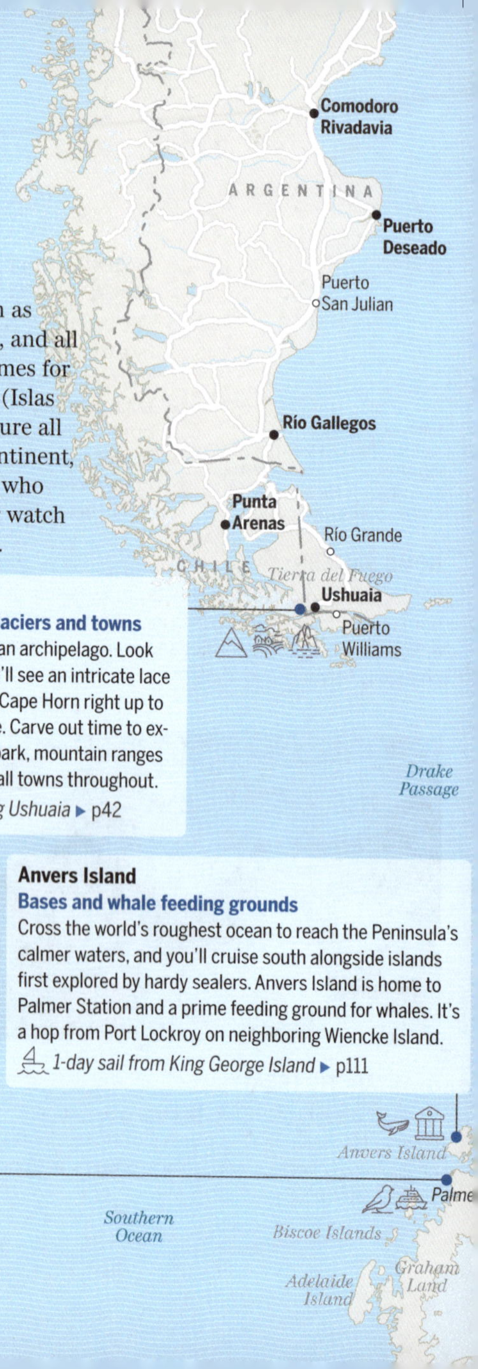

Tierra del Fuego

Myriad islands, glaciers and towns

Tierra del Fuego is an archipelago. Look at the map and you'll see an intricate lace of waterways from Cape Horn right up to Punta Arenas, Chile. Carve out time to explore the national park, mountain ranges and interesting small towns throughout.

Region surrounding Ushuaia ▸ p42

Anvers Island

Bases and whale feeding grounds

Cross the world's roughest ocean to reach the Peninsula's calmer waters, and you'll cruise south alongside islands first explored by hardy sealers. Anvers Island is home to Palmer Station and a prime feeding ground for whales. It's a hop from Port Lockroy on neighboring Wiencke Island.

1-day sail from King George Island ▸ p111

Petermann Island

Off the beaten track

Flirt with the Antarctic Circle at the world's southernmost gentoo colony at Petermann Island, one of the last stops of many cruises. Adélie penguins roost here, too. On a deep south cruise, continue to the Yalour Islands and islets strewn around Marguerite Bay.

2-day sail from Anvers Island ▸ p116

FROM LEFT: SEBASTIAN INTELISANO/SHUTTERSTOCK, ASHLEY COOPER/GETTY IMAGES, AMAZING AERIAL/ALAMY, MICHAEL NOLAN/ROBERTHARDING/GETTY IMAGES

Falkand Islands (Islas Malvinas)

Outdoors and inviting local life

Internal airplanes can fly you to the far-flung reaches of the fascinating Falkland Islands (Islas Malvinas) where you can explore rose-sanded beaches where penguins breed. An evening of pub-hopping in Stanley leads to stories for a lifetime (pictured below; p71).

1½-day sail from Ushuaia ▶ p72

South Atlantic Ocean

South Georgia Island

Incredible wildlife and whaling history

Abundant South Georgia Island is the domain of tussling, massive elephant seals (pictured above) and gamboling fur seals protecting their pups. Enormous colonies of penguin and seabirds dot its shores. Grytviken whaling station and its cemetery, where Ernest Shackleton is buried, take you back in time.

2-day sail from the Falkland Islands (Islas Malvinas) ▶ p84

West Falkland
Falkland Islands (UK)
Fox Bay
Stanley
East Falkland
Falkland Islands (Islas Malvinas)

Scotia Sea

South Georgia & South Sandwich Islands (UK)
South Georgia
Mt Paget
Grytviken

South Shetland Islands
Elephant Island
South Orkney Islands
Orcadas
Frei
Bransfield Strait
O'Higgins
Joinville Island
Esperanza
Marambio
James Ross Island
Antarctic Peninsula
Antarctica

Seymour Island

Fossils and dinosaur finds

Amid the cluster of islands on the northeast side of the Peninsula, Seymour Island's claim to fame is the many mega-fauna fossils discovered here, from the ages when giant creatures roamed Gondwanaland. Neighboring Vega and James Ross islands are tops for dinosaurs.

2-day sail from King George Island ▶ p128

0 500 km
0 250 miles

ICE SIZE

Antarctica is nicknamed The Ice.

The average thickness of its continental ice: 2160m

Largest iceberg to break off from Antarctica: A-23a, originally measuring about 4000 sq km

Size of smallest frazil ice, the needles/crystals that form in cold water: 1mm

FANTASTICAL ICE

Ah, how do you choose a favorite among Antarctica's many gorgeous ice formations and experiences? Simple, beautiful water is transformed into glitter dust, crackling discs, stripey twists and mammoth tabular floating islands. No matter the light conditions, you'll see something breathtaking, you'll hear them pop, clink and calve, you may even get to lick a piece from beside your Zodiac or kayak. Sensations for a lifetime.

Left Drygalski Ice Tongue (p159), Ross Sea **Right** Chinstrap penguins (p120) in midnight sun (p160) **Below** Ross Ice Shelf (p158), Ross Sea

→ ICE EXTRAVAGANZAS

Be wowed by light-struck ice formations (p105). Whether a wee floating berg, an enormous tabular iceberg or the crenelated tongue of a glacier, Antarctica has it all.

MOGENS TROLLE/SHUTTERSTOCK

SNOW ALGAE

Snow often has pink, red, orange, green, yellow or gray casts. It's snow algae! Single-celled organisms living atop snowfields, especially in the Antarctic Peninsula.

FROM LEFT: ROB FLETCHER/GETTY IMAGES, LUIS DAVILLA/GETTY IMAGES

↑ ICE SHELVES

Thundering icebergs calve from shelves like the Ross Ice Shelf (p158) and the Filchner-Ronne Ice Shelf (p128), where emperor penguins roost.

Best Icy Experiences

- **Look for icebergs near the Drygalski Ice Tongue.** (p159)
- **Explore the blue ice features around the interior fly-in camps.** (p194)
- **Crackle through the shimmering mirrors of ice and bergs floating on Cierva Cove, as whales breach.** (p105)
- **Sail into the pack ice that has crushed many a ship in the Weddell Sea.** (p126)
- **Go winter dog-sledding or skiing in the Tierra Mayor Valley north of Ushuaia.** (p52)

ROSS ICE SHELF

The thinnest part of the Ross Ice Shelf – a mere 100m thick – faces the sea. Inland, where the glaciers meet it, the slab can be as much as 1000m thick. The whole floating shelf is an astounding 500,000 sq km.

REMOTE **REACHES**

Even on Antarctica there are places that only the most fortunate or intrepid get to experience. It is a rare day when a non-scientist comes to most East Antarctic bases, and some subantarctic islands are visited just a couple of times a year. Adventures onto the Polar Plateau usually find your group all alone.

ANDREW PEACOCK/GETTY IMAGES

Left King penguins, Macquarie Island (p176), Ross Sea **Right** Iceberg, Antarctic Peninsula (p92) **Below** McMurdo Dry Valleys (p169), Ross Sea

→ WINTERING IN ANTARCTICA

Wintering on an Antarctic base, especially the South Pole (p180), is a life-changing experience. Isolating for up to eight months produces radical effects.

ROSS ICE SHELF

This towering sheet of ice, rising from the Ross Sea, was a daunting obstacle to Antarctic explorers. In fact, it was formerly known simply as 'The Barrier.'

FROM LEFT: BMJ/SHUTTERSTOCK, COPYRIGHT JEFF MILLER/GETTY IMAGES

↑ DRY VALLEYS

Empty but for microscopic life forms, mummified seals, bizarre lakes and wind-sculpted ventifacts...only a very lucky few drop in (via helicopter; p169) on the other-worldly Ross Sea Dry Valleys.

Best Remote Experiences

- **Parade through the blue ice of the interior at Schirmacher Oasis or Union Glacier.** (p195)
- **Go hunting for dinosaurs and giant fossils in the Weddell Sea.** (p126)
- **Sail below the Antarctic Circle to Marguerite Bay.** (p117)
- **Adventure to Cape Adare for historic huts and Antarctica's largest Adélie penguin colony.** (p150)
- **Visit roosting royal penguins at their only home, Macquarie Island.** (p176)

↓ Gentoo Penguins

On southerly islands and the Peninsula, gentoos lay two eggs from October to December. Further north, egg-laying occurs as early as July.

← White Desert

Antarctica's interior, despite its ice cap, is the world's driest desert, since the extreme cold freezes water vapor out of the air.

The annual snowfall on the polar plateau is equivalent to less than 5cm of rain.

Average Coastal/Peninsula Temperature: 0°C (32°F)

South Pole Temperature: -36°C (-33°F)

The winter sea ice breaks up.

Antarctica in NOVEMBER

The Antarctic Peninsula (p92) is the consistently warmest part of the continent year-round, so it attracts the majority of the wildlife.

↗ Emperor Incubation

Emperor penguin incubation averages 66 days, and chicks become independent between November and January.

↓ Chinstrap Penguins

Chinstrap penguins lay two eggs in November and chicks fledge by early March.

Whales start migrating into the region to feed.

October and November penguins begin their courtship and lay eggs.

Light-mantled albatross finish laying eggs in November.

Packing Notes

Consider specialty photographic equipment, like polarizing filters, and bring a spare camera battery – cold drains them quickly.

Antarctic blizzards are common, but are usually violently blown snow which has fallen over years and never melted, not falling snow.

↗ Albatross Incubation

Wandering albatross lay eggs from mid-December through January, and begin their incubation of approximately 74–85 days.

↖ Midnight Sun

Expect up to 20 hours of sunlight each day, and the main influx of Antarctic visitors during the height of summer.

Average Coastal/Peninsula Temperature: 1°C (34°F)

South Pole Temperature: -20°C to -15°C (-4°F to 5°F)

Penguins hatch eggs and feed chicks; seabirds soar.

Antarctica in DECEMBER

FROM LEFT: WOLFGANG KAEHLER/LIGHTROCKET VIA GETTY IMAGES, LIZ CARLSON, MARTIN MECNAROWSKI/SHUTTERSTOCK, N8TUREGRL/GETTY IMAGES, LOUIELEA/SHUTTERSTOCK. BACKGROUND: BART FIGAS/SHUTTERSTOCK

↓ Falkland Celebrations

Holiday events like the Winter Ball and New Year raft race kick off in Stanley in the Falkland Islands (Islas Malvinas).

← South Georgia Wildlife

Peak wildlife season begins in South Georgia and the abundance of seals (pictured), seabirds and penguins continues through January.

Demand for tours peaks during mid-December through January.

Fur seal pupping takes place.

Summer solstice is Dec 21, the longest day of Antarctica's year.

Days are the warmest the continent will see.

Packing Notes

Include a few of your finest clothes for holiday events on board your ship.

↘ Calm January

The strongest winds on Earth, katabatics achieve velocities up to 320km/h. Winds on the plateau, by contrast, are usually very light. Generally, it's windiest in June, calmest in January.

↓ Hot Soak

Bring a bathing suit and water shoes (old tennis shoes will do) if you are going to the thermal waters at Deception Island (p100).

Average Coastal/Peninsula Temperature: 2°C (36°F)

South Pole Temperature: -29°C (-20°F)

Antarctica in JANUARY

FROM LEFT: THOMAS BARWICK/GETTY IMAGES, MIKE HILL/GETTY IMAGES, EITAN ABRAMOVICH/AFP VIA GETTY IMAGES, STU SHAW/SHUTTERSTOCK, NANCY PAUWELS/GETTY IMAGES. BACKGROUND: OLEKSANDR MATSIBURA/SHUTTERSTOCK

↓ Polar Camping & Kayaking

Stable weather allows for outdoor activities like overnight ice camping beneath the midnight sun and kayaking through newly opened iceberg channels.

Winter Weather

In coldest July, the mean temperature in Antarctic's interior is -70°C to -40°C (-94°C to -40°C). The coastal temperature in winter is -32°C to -15°C (-26°F to 5°F).

↖ Reflective Power

The continent's permanent ice cover reflects about 80% of the sun's radiation back into space, contributing to its frigid temps.

Peak numbers of whales in the Antarctic Peninsula and surrounding areas.

It's the height of the feeding season with giant krill swarms.

Packing Notes

Don't forget a windproof and waterproof jacket and trousers (p230), though some high-end operators will provide a parka for you.

Cruises later in the season may be less crowded; however, the longer you wait to go, the more wildlife will have already headed out to sea.

↓ Ripe Berries in the Falklands

In the Falkland Islands, pale pink and very sweet teaberries or diddle-dees (pictured) ripen and can be eaten fresh.

↖ Royal Penguins

Macquarie Island royal penguins lay two eggs (the first of which is discarded) in October with chicks fledging by February.

Average Coastal/Peninsula Temperature: -3°C to 0°C (27°F to 32°F)

South Pole Temperature: -42°C to -37°C (-44°F to -35°F)

Antarctica in FEBRUARY

FROM LEFT: AGAMI PHOTO AGENCY/SHUTTERSTOCK, GALINA SAVINA/SHUTTERSTOCK, PETER MACDIARMID/GETTY IMAGES, EVENFH/SHUTTERSTOCK, DAVID MERRON PHOTOGRAPHY/GETTY IMAGES. BACKGROUND: FRANK GÜNTHER/GETTY IMAGES

↓ Camp Sports Week

The Falkland Islands (Islas Malvinas) hold their Camp Sports Week across the islands at the end of February, with dog trials, sheep shearing and other entertainment.

↖ Sea Ice

Antarctic sea-ice cover varies from a minimum of 4 million sq km in February to a maximum of 20 million sq km in September.

February to March is prime time for whale-watching, as they are abundant and relaxed.

Adélie, gentoo and chinstrap adult penguins molt and chicks fledge.

Packing Notes

See if you'll need an electrical adapter for your cruise ship. Bring seasickness solutions for the crossing.

7 Things to Know About ANTARCTICA

INSIDER TIPS TO HIT THE GROUND RUNNING

1 Food is Part of the Package

You'll eat aboard your ship or at the base camp run by your tour operator, and it's included in the price. Operators describe the style of food in their promotional material, and on luxury cruises you can get perks like room service or bespoke meals. If you have specific dietary needs, it's vital to flag them before booking. And no, you don't have to eat pemmican.

▶ See more about pemmican on p153

2 Partying Under the Midnight Sun

Cruise ships usually have bar and drinking options, though the price of alcohol may not be included in the tour price (check in advance). Larger ships will have more options, though life aboard ship is usually fun-loving, no matter the size. Research stations can have raucous nightlife, with the 24-hour sunshine of summer or the extreme isolation of winter, but most tourists won't gain access to the shore-side bars.

▶ See more about base life on p111

3 Adventure Add-Ons

When booking, consider whether your ship offers activities like sea kayaking (usually OK for beginners), scuba diving, or camping and mountain-climbing add-ons. Some offer flights to the interior and the chance to ski or trek.

▶ See more about add-on activities on p219

4 Action Underway

Onboard lectures, films and events are the main entertainment at sea. They usually offer excellent background information for excursions. Some ships have gyms.

▶ See more about life onboard on p220

5 Kids on Board & Screen Time

Children are still relatively rare visitors to Antarctica, but the kids we met loved the amazing landscapes and wildlife – especially the penguin and whale spotting. Sea time can become tedious if they're the only kids on board – it helps to travel as a larger family. You can also help them learn about Antarctic topics before and during the voyage and encourage them to question ship staff. Meredith Hooper is a great author of children's Antarctic stories. Most boats are kitted out with board games and the like.

If your kid or teen counts on their device, beware that internet services vary: some ships have decent in-cabin wi-fi, others use a common computer. The internet service can be included in your tour price, or come at an exorbitant cost. Ask your operator. Speed is slower than on land, and coverage breaks up sometimes. Standard mobile phones don't work at sea or in Antarctica.

6 Photography

Want that great shot of a whale fluking or a penguin leaping from an iceberg? Most cruises have photographers documenting the trip, offer a final slideshow, and gift you images, while others charge for images and videos. To master the craft yourself, book a cruise where the photographer is also an onshore guide or offers tips and classes.

▶ See more about photography on p164

7 Dress for Comfort

Conditions are rough in Antarctica, so bring layers – from long underwear and sock liners to heavy parkas, if your tour doesn't provide one. Plan for wind- and sea-lashed boat decks and sub-zero temperatures on the Ice. Emphasize waterproof, quick-dry and perspiration-wicking materials. Shoot for practical – penguins don't care about fashion.

▶ See more about what to pack on p230

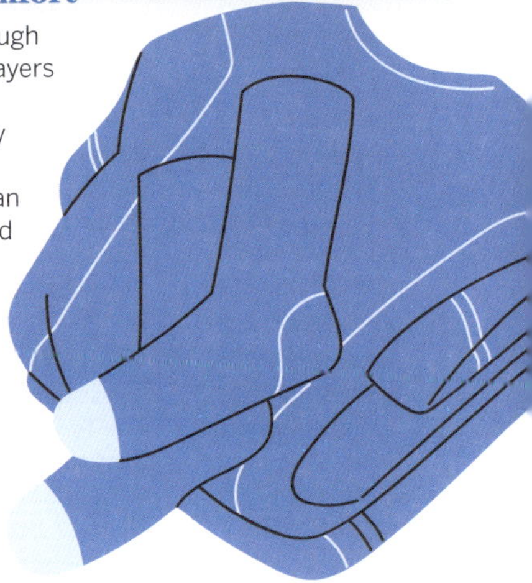

Read, Listen, Watch & Follow

READ

Endurance: Shackleton's Incredible Voyage (Alfred Lansing; 1959) Page-turner survival story.

Dispatches from Continent Seven (Rebecca Priestley; 2016) Science and discovery over time.

The Penguin Book of Penguins (Peter Fretwell & Lisa Fretwell; 2025) All about the beloved bird.

The Worst Journey in the World (Apsley Cherry-Garrard; 1922) Profound account of midwinter haul to Cape Crozier.

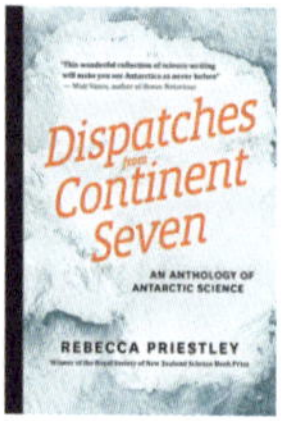

LISTEN

The Seventh Continent (Sounds of Space; 2024) Music, sounds and interviews recorded on and inspired by Antarctica.

Antarctic Symphony (2001) Sir Peter Maxwell Davies' (pictured) Symphony No 8, inspired by the composer's trip to The Ice.

A Voyage to Antarctica Podcast by UK Antarctic Heritage Trust interviewing scientists, artists and more.

Scott's Music Box: Music from the Terra Nova (Various Artists; 2012) Compilation of music played on Robert Falcon Scott's doomed expedition.

GARY DOAK/ALAMY

Against the Odds Season 6, *Endurance: Surviving Antarctica*, details Shackleton's perilous 1914–17 expedition. Season 56, *Alone in Antarctica*, is Douglas Mawson's harrowing experience exploring the Antarctic coast.

WATCH

La Marche de l'Empereur (March of the Penguins; 2005; pictured top) Iconic Oscar-winning documentary of emperor penguin life.

The Thing (1982; Kurt Russell pictured bottom) Thrills and chills on an isolated base. Skip the lesser remake from 2011.

Encounters at the End of the World (2007) Werner Herzog filming McMurdo Station staff and scientists.

The Great White Silence (1924) Silent footage of Scott's *Terra Nova* expedition.

South (1919) Original documentary directed by Frank Hurley about Shackleton's expedition.

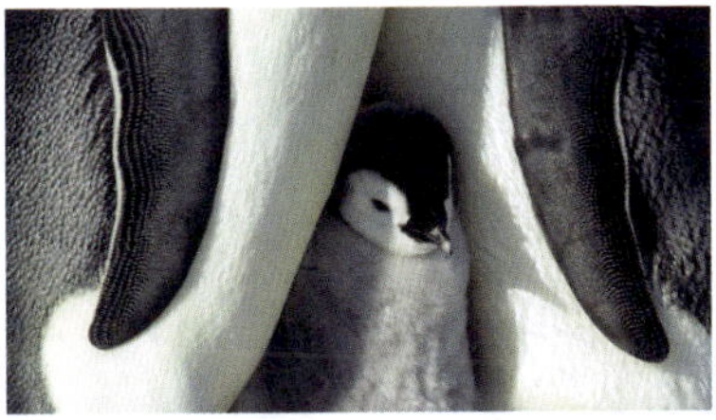

PICTURELUX / THE HOLLYWOOD ARCHIVE/ALAMY

COLLECTION CHRISTOPHEL/ALAMY

FOLLOW

@simplyantarctica
Fun dispatches from the Ice.

@mattykjordan
Life in Antarctica with humor and footage.

@jvn.photo
Landscape and wildlife photography, including Antarctica.

@polarwomen
Female scientists at both of the Poles.

Cool Antarctica
(coolantarctica.com) Antarctic trivia, interesting facts and pics.

USHUAIA

MOUNTAINS | ADVENTURE | HISTORY

RESEARCHED BY ALEXIS AVERBUCK

USHUAIA
Trip Builder

The southernmost extreme of the Americas, the windswept archipelago of Tierra del Fuego is as alluring as it is moody – by turns beautiful, ancient and fascinating. Ushuaia takes full advantage of its end-of-the-world status, and many Antarctica-bound vessels call into its port.

In winter, go dog sledding or skiing in the central **Tierra Mayor Valley** (p52)
20 min from Ushuaia

Adventure to mountaintop glaciers like **Vinciguerra** (p53)
30 min from Ushuaia

Take in indigenous and maritime histories at **Ushuaia's museums** (p46)

Chug along on a steam train through **Parque Nacional Tierra del Fuego** (p42)
20 min from Ushuaia

Day-trip through the **Beagle Channel** (p40) for a kaleidoscope of wildlife
2 hr from Ushuaia

CLOCKWISE FROM TOP LEFT: PEPPELR/GETTY IMAGES, SUNSINGER/SHUTTERSTOCK, TICIANA GIEHL/SHUTTERSTOCK, PROCY_AB/GETTY IMAGES. PREVIOUS SPREAD: MEUNIERD/SHUTTERSTOCK

Practicalities

BRESTER IRINA/SHUTTERSTOCK

ARRIVING

Ushuaia International Airport Taxis to/from the modern airport (pictured), 4km southwest of downtown, cost approximately US$10.

Car and bus With Argentina's half of Tierra del Fuego spanning just over 21,000 sq km, the Ruta 3 highway connects the Chilean border with San Sebastián in the north, sweeping down to Ushuaia. Reliable minibus shuttles (see schedules at *turismoushuaia.com*) connect Ushuaia and Río Grande with a stop at Tolhuin. Buses also go to Punta Arenas in Chile from Monday to Saturday.

HOW MUCH FOR A

Empanada US$1

Pint of craft beer US$5

National park entry US$5–22

WHEN TO GO

OCT–NOV
Boats for Antarctica begin heading south and temperatures start to climb.

DEC–FEB
Warmest months, best for hiking, penguin-watching and *estancia* (ranch) visits.

MAR–JUN
Fly-fishing season ends in April and winter arrives.

JUL–SEP
Peak winter, optimal for skiing, snowboarding and dogsledding.

GETTING AROUND

On foot If you base yourself in the center all the museums and most restaurants are close to Av San Martín and tour operators pick you up from your accommodations for day trips; boat tours depart from the **Puerto Turístico**.

Shuttle buses The **bus station** (Terminal de Ómnibus de Ushuaia) serves destinations such as Glaciar Martial, Tren del Fin del Mundo, the winter centers and the trailheads of Laguna Esmeralda and other walks.

Car and taxi Two or four wheels are optimal for exploring further afield. Taxis (app Taxis Clientes Ushuaia; +54 2901-422007) publish set fares to Harberton, Almanza and other destinations outside the city.

TOP: LARISA BLINOVA/SHUTTERSTOCK
BOTTOM: LEONARD ZHUKOVSKY/SHUTTERSTOCK

EATING & DRINKING

Ushuaia is known for for its king crab (pictured top right) cooked to perfection, its mouth-watering *ceviche* (cured raw fish) and its juicy lamb slow-grilled in traditional *asado* (barbecue) fashion. Vegetarians and vegans, beware: farm-fresh fruits and vegetables are difficult to find outside of the summer months.

Yerba mate, or *mate* (pronounced mah-tay) for short, is a tea with about as much caffeine as coffee. You'll see people everywhere armed with hollow gourds filled with the loose-leaf tea, sipping it through a *bombilla* (filtered straw). Geographically competitive drinkers note: the southern-most bar in the world is not here, but on a Ukrainian base in Antarctica.

Best microbrew
Patagonia Brewing Co (p62; pictured bottom right)

Must-try medialunas
Ana y Juana (p60)

CONNECT & FIND YOUR WAY

Wi-fi Free hotspots abound. If you have data roaming or buy a local SIM card, signal disappears in the mountains.

Navigation Most visitor services are on or near Av San Martín, two blocks from the waterfront and paralleling the Beagle Channel. Av Maipú becomes Malvinas Argentinas west of the cemetery, then turns into RN 3, continuing 12km to Parque Nacional Tierra del Fuego.

WHERE TO STAY

Reserve well ahead if you're planning a visit from January to early March. Check when booking for free arrival transfers. In winter, rates drop slightly and some places close, though visits at this time are becoming popular.

Neighborhood	Pro/Con
Central Ushuaia	Super convenient to navigate on foot and near most services. More crowded and touristic.
Surrounding hills	Sweeping vistas of the Beagle Channel and near mountain walks. Require a taxi into town.
Estancias	Unique, rural getaways which give a real sense of Tierra del Fuego. Remote.

DRESS FOR EVERYTHING

As Tierra del Fuego famously has four seasons in an hour, adopt 'onion dressing' by wearing layers you can peel off to suit the climate.

MONEY

Banks on Avs Maipú and San Martín have ATMs and cards are widely accepted. Food and drink in the touristic center is similar in price to the United States and Europe.

01 Beagle Channel WILDERNESS

ISLANDS | PENGUINS | LIGHTHOUSE

The closest you can get to Antarctica without leaving Argentina, and arguably a main reason to visit Tierra del Fuego in itself, the archipelago of the fabled Beagle Channel is home to captivating Antarctic marine wildlife, iconic sights and subpolar fauna unmatched anywhere else on the planet.

FILIPPOBACCI/GETTY IMAGES

How to

Getting here Boat tours depart from the **Puerto Turístico** twice a day, in the mornings and afternoons.

When to go Tours operate in the warmer summer months when you'll have the best chance to spot wildlife.

Get a penguin pic Don't forget to bring your long lens...most boats don't land at the penguin colony, so you'll be shooting from afar.

R.M. NUNES/SHUTTERSTOCK

Above left Isla Bridges **Below left** Magellanic penguin, Isla Martillo

Polar Wildlife on Subantarctic Isles

Island walk Book a tour with a walk to breathe in the crisp marine air on **Isla Bridges**, which carbon dating has shown to have been settled by the indigenous Yaghan people (p48) – there's a replica hut and information about the indigenous history and endemic fauna set against the scintillating 360-degree panorama of surrounding Ushuaia and Isla Navarino.

Penguin spotting During summer boats tour to **Isla Martillo** *pinguinera* (penguin colony). Wildlife watchers will also catch glimpses of whales and seals on their sailings along the mountainous coastline of this southernmost point of the Americas. **Piratour** (piratour.net) is the only agency with permission to walk on the island near the penguins and to tour here year-round. Magellanic penguins migrate to Peninsula Valdés when the temperature drops, but Papua penguins stay put. King penguins have recently been spotted on Isla Martillo, too.

Seals and seabirds Say hello to the South American sea lions of **Isla Alicia**, delight in the cormorant colony of **Isla de los Pájaros** (also replete with barking pinnipeds when we visited) and survey the iconic, century-old **Les Eclaireurs Lighthouse**. It's the site of the 1930 *Monte Cervantes* shipwreck, occasionally visible when the tide is low.

Get underwater Ushuaia Divers (facebook.com/ushuaiadivers) leads scuba diving in the Beagle Channel where you can swim with sea lions and explore the notorious array of shipwrecks.

Chilean Getaway

Even the southernmost city in the world faces competition: in 2019, Chile declared little Puerto Williams a city, vying for the title from Ushuaia. It's on Isla Navarino, just 5km across the channel from Argentina's Puerto Almanza, and day-trip boats go from Ushuaia each morning from November to March.

Reaching Isla Navarino year-round is possible via Punta Arenas in Chile. DAP Airlines runs flights, while the Yaghan ferry voyages for 30 hours. On Navarino, you'll find the world's largest Yaghan community, the Dientes de Navarino hike – part of which is named after Lonely Planet writer Clem Lindenmayer, who pioneered the route – and Cape Horn beyond.

02 Parque Nacional Tierra DEL FUEGO

WILDERNESS | WALKS | TRAIN

Spanning nearly 700 sq km, Parque Nacional Tierra del Fuego, with its subpolar sea, snowcapped mountains, glacial lakes and pony-grazing valleys, is the most-visited site in the region. Explore on a historic steam train or stroll among foxes on coastal trails.

GUAXINIM/SHUTTERSTOCK

How to

Getting here Organized tours come here, and buses leave from Ushuaia's **bus station** on the hour each morning. There are six stops, including Bahía Ensenada Zaratiegui, Alakush Visitors Center and Lapataia Bay. Or it's an easy drive 11km west from town.

Get tickets Buy in advance (trendelfindelmundo.com.ar) or as part of a tour. Park entry is separate (argentina.gob.ar).

Play in the park Summertime canoeing is the only official activity allowed in the park, and you can camp overnight.

FABIDECIRIA/SHUTTERSTOCK

Tren del Fin del Mundo

This evocative steam locomotive winding between lenga forests and snowcapped mountains lives up to the hype. It's a recreation of the journey made by the city's first immigrant wave – prisoners exiled to the turn-of-the-20th-century penal colony (p46) of Ushuaia to work in the forests to build the city. You'll start at the faux-period **Tren del Fin del Mundo Station** and choochoo into the Parque Nacional Tierra del Fuego, looping into parts that are inaccessible by road. Insightful commentary about the prison history of Ushuaia in four languages is inevitably upstaged by the rolling views of wild horses grazing tundra snaked by glacial streams. You'll stop at **La Macarena Waterfall** for a short walk up to its edge. The comedic prisoner photo ops are a

ALEXANDRE.ROSA/SHUTTERSTOCK

Wildlife Watching

When you hike, in the quiet, you'll likely encounter grey and red foxes, (non-native) beavers and myriad birds. Try spotting the Alakush flightless steamer duck, which lends its name to the visitors center, and guanacos and condors along the Cerro Guanaco trail. Whatever you do, don't feed the animals.

Above left Laguna del Caminante (p45)
Below left Bahía Lapataia (p45)
Above Condor, Isla de los Pájaros (p41), Beagle Channel

bit awkward, but the panoramic mountain-topped surroundings are magnificent.

Hiking Forests & Mountains

The park's well-maintained trails range from coastal and lake walks to arduous mountain hikes and short waterfall detours. You'll tramp through lenga forests fringing glacial waters beneath towering snowcapped mountains.

For example, the **Senda Costera Trail** (closed May to December) leads from **Bahía Ensenada Zaratiegui** to **Lago Acigami**, which extends into Chile. It traces along the iconic western coastline of the Beagle Channel through forests, hidden coves and beaches. Look out for raised mounds of earth along the way – these could be middens, left by the Yaghans who dwelt here.

The **Cerro Guanaco Trail** is a challenging 6km (one-way) uphill mountain hike to binary views of the sea and Fuegian Andes. To embark on this you must register with the **Alakush Visitors Center** first.

Top Tips

- You can stop into the **National Park Office** in Ushuaia to get maps and ideas for hiking and camping. The park entrance kiosk also distributes a basic map.
- Camping is free and first-come-first-served at Bahía Ensenada, Laguna Verde, Río Pipo and Bahía Ensenada Zaratiegui.
- Some hiking routes close during winter.
- Bring bug spray for summer walks.
- Take the Tren del Fin del Mundo one way, then hike or join a tour to explore the park before or after. It's not particularly worth it to buy 'Premium' or 'VIP' tickets on the train as all of the windows are about the same.

Left Bahía Ensenada Zaratiegui
Below Tren del Fin del Mundo (p43)

The stroll to **Río Pipo waterfall** is an easy 15-minute (0.8km) ascent, while the trail up the mountains to **Lago Superior** and **Laguna del Caminante** starts in the park and takes several days.

Sparkling Lakes & Bays

Opening like a lunar crater is the perfect sphere of **Lago Acigami** (now renamed Lago Roca) – a pristine expanse of glacial water sentinelled by imposing ice-capped mountain escarpments and Chile to the west. Trails lead around the crescent of pebble beach – follow it to fruition on the **Hito XXIV Trail** to reach the border with Chile. Relax on log benches lakeside en route.

Further south, follow short trails of 10 minutes or so around the wooden walkways lining **Bahía Lapataia**, at the end of the Pan-American Highway (p56).

Refuge at the End of the World

Take a break at the spacious **Alakush Visitors Center**. Their small exhibition explains the glacial, anthropological and constructed evolution of the national park. Kick back in its roomy cafeteria with panoramic views and a fire. Seek out the space to the back right with views of the ice-capped mountains fringing the **Lapataia River**.

03 History & Culture in USHUAIA

HISTORY | ANTARCTIC EXPLORERS | PENAL COLONY

Step inside the city's major museums and you can spend days exploring regional culture and history, learning about the deeper aspects of life in Tierra del Fuego. Plan extra time for tours by a Yaghan author and lecturer or at the expansive museum set in a penal colony, which includes extensive exhibits on Antarctic exploration.

FROM TOP: ALEXANDRE ROSA/SHUTTERSTOCK, NTNU VITENSKAPSMUSEET/WIKIMEDIA/CC BY 2.0

How to

Getting here All of the museums are an easy walk to the eastern end of central Ushuaia.

Come back for more Tickets to the museums, Marítimo (museomaritimo.com) and Fin del Mundo (mfm.tierradelfuego.gob.ar), allow reentry over three days.

See it all Two wings of the Museo Marítimo & Museo del Presidio, including the maritime arts, only open in the afternoon from 3pm to 7pm.

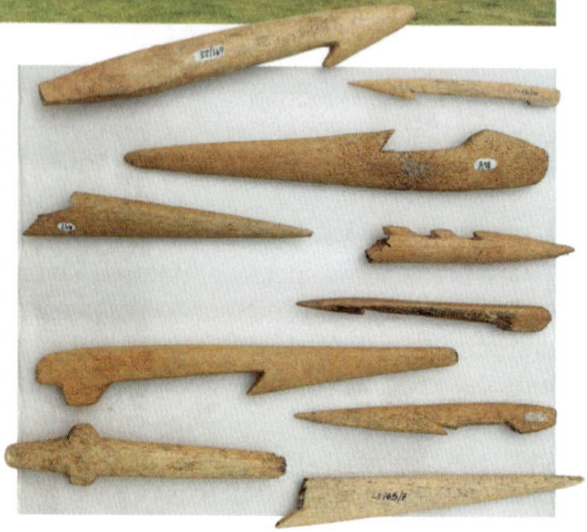

Prison-turned-museum The sprawling asterisk-shaped building on the eastern edge of Ushuaia's center now houses the **Museo Marítimo & Museo del Presidio**. Convicts were sent here in 1906 to build this national prison designed for 380 inmates, which was finished in 1920, but held up to 800 before closing in 1947. It's a panopticon – prisoners could be observed from the hub of the wheel-like shape. Now you can walk the tiny cells, where each of the five spokes is devoted to a different local fascination from maritime and Yaghan history to Antarctic expeditions – complete with ship models. Famous prisoners include author Ricardo Rojas and anarchist Simón Radowitzky.

Remains of the world's narrowest-gauge freight train, which transported prisoners between town and work stations, sit in the courtyard. Guided tours in Spanish are at 11.30am, 4.30pm and 6.30pm.

Local culture and natural history Delve into the **Museo del Fin del Mundo** in two veteran buildings on Av Maipú. The first at No 173 was built in 1903, and was formerly a bank. Close to the port, it contains exhibits on Fuegian natural history, stuffed birdlife, photos of indigenous people and the early penal colony. Walk east to No 465 to find the second, **La Antigua Casa de Gobierno**, built in 1890. It covers the sinking of *Monte Cervantes* in 1930 through original footage and first-person accounts.

Above left Museo Marítimo & Museo del Presidio **Below left** Harpoon heads, Museo del Fin del Mundo

Yaghan History

Every day at the Museo del Fin del Mundo, lecturer Victor Vargas Filgueira, a member of Ushuaia's small Paliakoala indigenous community and son of Cristina Calderón, the last Yaghan speaker in the world (d 2022), gives talks in Spanish about the region's indigenous history and culture at 11am. Ask to see his basketry and handicrafts before exploring the absorbing exhibits on Antarctic wildlife and the human history of Tierra del Fuego.

If you read Spanish, you can learn more in his book, *Mi Sangre Yagán* (My Yaghan Blood), available through **Boutique del Libro**.

The Yaghan People of Tierra del Fuego

THE WORLD'S SOUTHERNMOST INDIGENOUS PEOPLE

Part of traveling to Tierra del Fuego is searching for clues to its rich cultural past. Souvenir shops sell a postcard of abstract intrigue: there's a naked man painted black. Fine horizontal white stripes cross his body from chest to foot. His face remains covered. So, what's this all about?

HISTORIC ILLUSTRATIONS/ALAMY

Left A Yaghan person **Centre** A replica Yaghan hut **Right** Cristina Calderón, the last Yaghan speaker in the world (p47)

The Yaghan (or Yámana) people were a nomadic group whose members thrived in Tierra del Fuego's brutal weather conditions. They are the southernmost indigenous people in the world and were historically hunter-gatherers who used canoes to fish, gather shellfish, hunt, and collect mushrooms and vegetation on the archipelago.

The Yaghan people didn't maintain permanent shelters and they believed that the natural oil of their skin was better protection than soaking-wet animal fur. This all changed when Europeans entered the area.

European Interference

In 1870 the British-based South American Missionary Society set its sights on the Yaghan people. Charles Darwin branded them 'the lowest form of humanity on earth.' Missionary Thomas Bridges didn't agree. After years among them, he created a Yaghan–English dictionary in the late 19th century to translate their unique language.

The mission made Ushuaia its first permanent Fuegian outpost, but the Yaghan, who had survived 6000 years without contact, were vulnerable to foreign-brought illnesses and faced increasing infringement by sealers, settlers and gold prospectors. Four Yaghan, including a teenager named Orundellico who was then dubbed 'Jemmy Button,' were kidnapped by the naval captain Robert FitzRoy and shipped back to England to be 'educated' and paraded around. One of the kidnapped people died of disease, and after months of public criticism, FitzRoy agreed to return the others to their homeland. Orundellico (Jemmy Button) returned on the *Beagle* with Darwin.

MAURITIUS IMAGES GMBH/ALAMY

RIDINGHOOD/ALAMY

Nowadays you can find out more about the tribe's legacy – beyond the shell mounds that still dot the coastline – at **Museo Marítimo & Museo del Presidio** (p47), **Museo del Fin del Mundo** (p47) and **Alakush Visitors Center** (p44).

Fuegian Rites of Passage

For people who lived exposed to the elements, dependent on their wits and courage, Hain initiation ceremonies were very meaningful. Those of the seafaring Yaghan were surprisingly similar to those of the fierce northern neighbors they wanted little to do with, the nomadic hunters called Selk'nam (or Ona to the Yaghan). Both celebrated a male rite of passage that reenacted a great upheaval when the men stole the women's secrets to gain power over them. In the Kina, Yaghan men interpreted the spirits by painting their bodies with black carbon and striped or dotted patterns that used the region's white and red clays. The anthropologist Anna Chapman documented the phenomenon extensively, with the last known Hain ceremony taking place in 1923.

Captured on Film

Among the spate of anti-colonial Westerns released in 2023, *Los Colonos*, depicting the Selk'nam genocide led by José Menéndez, received multiple awards. It followed Chile's 2018 entry to the Academy Awards, *Blanco en Blanco*, which also centered around the hunting of the indigenous people of northern Isla Grande.

Skip the movie *Tierra del Fuego*, based around the brutal massacre led by Julian Popper, and instead read the book it's modeled on. Francisco Coloane's excellent short story collection hinges around south Patagonia's short-lived gold rush under the so-called King of Paramo, Popper.

The Hain Ceremony

Practiced by all the indigenous peoples of Tierra del Fuego, the Hain ceremony is honored in museums, municipal statues and the names of restaurants, accommodations and even a theater across Isla Grande. The days- or weeks-long initiation ceremony saw adolescent boys learn to fish, hunt and engage in spiritual development under the guidance of community elders who imparted their wisdom in a specially built ceremonial hut. The boys were decorated using body and face paints, as well as costumes made from down and fur, and the rite of passage was accompanied by special chants.

04 ICY Adventures

GLACIERS | SPORTS | FLIGHTSEEING

Among Ushuaia's greatest lures, its surrounding glaciers, formed over millennia, present a taster to its neighbor 1000km south, Antarctica. Set in the cradle of the Fuegian Andes, hours- or days-long mountain adventures begin in valleys within the city or a mere 20-minute drive from Ushuaia.

FREDLYFISH4/SHUTTERSTOCK

How to

Self-drive If you have your own wheels, the roads to winter sports centers are well-maintained and easy to navigate.

Climb glaciers Experienced mountain guides **Compañia de Guías de Patagonia** adjust itineraries to your abilities and interests.

Drink at Cerro Martial **La Cabaña Casa de Té** (p60) and **La Cabaña Beer Point** (p62) are excellent, but if you can't make it up the mountain, Glaciar Martial provides most of Ushuaia's water.

DMITRY_SAPAROV/GETTY IMAGES

Martial Mountain Magic

Snake up the winding mountain road from central Ushuaia to the snowcapped peak of **Cerro Martial** and you'll see Beagle Channel views sweeping below. Once you get up to the resort base, take the well-signposted hike to the cirque glacier – it's relatively easy after an initially steep stretch. The round-trip trek takes around three hours. Alas, the panoramic views are slightly more impressive than those of the glacier itself, which has receded in recent years.

LUJAN AGUSTI/BLOOMBERG VIA GETTY IMAGES

At the resort base itself, kit yourself out at hiking and snow outfitters, and in winter, **Escuela de Esquí Ushuaia** runs ski and snowboarding classes. The **Centro de Montana Glaciar Martial** in the former chairlift station offers guided treks and night hikes. Continue the adventure by coursing the nine ziplines of **Canopy Ushuaia** or ski cross-country

Take to the Air

Get a bird's-eye view over wondrous inaccessible sights. Soar over **Laguna Esmeralda** and **Monte Olivia** then alight atop **Alvear**, where you can heli-ski, too. Overfly **Península Mitre** to **Isla de los Estados** (and the lighthouse that inspired Jules Verne's *The Lighthouse at the End of the World*) and Cape Horn. **HeliUshuaia** flies choppers, **Aeroclub Ushuaia** airplanes.

Above left Cerro Martial **Below left** Ski resort, Cerro Castor (p53) **Above** Isla de los Estados

with Francisco Jerman, part of veteran **Club Andino Ushuaia** (clubandinoushuaia.com.ar), with whom you can book a snowboarding, mountain-climbing or ice-skating class.

Taxis down the mountain are on standby and buses leave on the hour during afternoons.

Frozen Adventures at the Winter Centers

The **Tierra Mayor Valley**, like so much of the lowlands lining the southern tip of Tierra del Fuego, was formed from a giant glacier that broke off from the Darwin range 25,000 years ago, molding the flat valley that so dramatically affords access to surrounding peaks.

If you visit between June and September, you can enter a Narnian winter wonderland by husky-sledding through lenga forests from the **Centro Invernal Tierra Mayor** or ice-climbing a frozen waterfall.

Snowmobile through the 5 hectares of snow-swept valley at **Llanos del Castor**, then

Mountain Tours

Compañia de Guías de Patagonia (companiadeguiasdepatagonia.tur.ar) Go-to experts on local climbs who tailor trips to you.

Arpon Trekking (arpontrekking.com) Family-run agency leading small-group tours to the Vinciguerra and Ojo del Albino glaciers.

Canal Tierra del Fuego (canalfun.com) Long-established operator with an array of small-group day hikes and tours.

Patagon Mountain Agency (patagonmountainagency.com) Agency steering intrepid – and varied – day hikes around the glaciers, ice climbing and more.

Terramar Turismo (terramar.tur.ar) Offers everything from national park to Beagle Channel trips.

Native Adventure Rents out bikes and e-bikes, plus arranges canoeing and other outdoor activities.

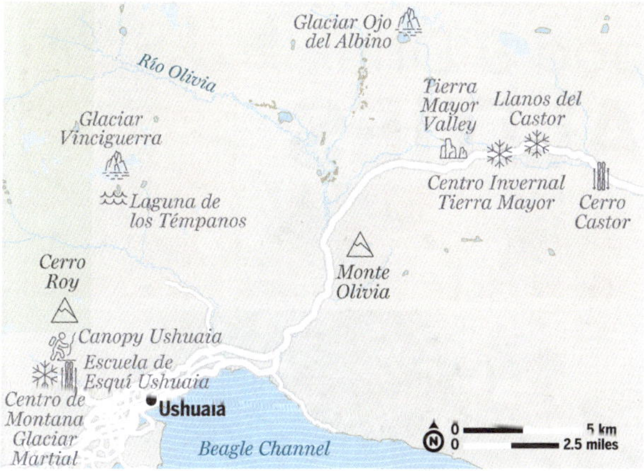

Left Glaciar Ojo del Albino
Below Entrance to ice caves, Glaciar Vinciguerra

hit the 19 slopes of the only full-scale ski resort in the extreme south of the Americas, **Cerro Castor**. This sophisticated enterprise of a former Olympian has après-piste DJs and lodgings. After dark, twinkling lights and hot chocolate heighten the contrast of night sky and snow.

All have homey restaurants serving excellent *parrilla* (grill foods).

Remote Glaciers

The most challenging of Ushuaia's entry-level day hikes are to the region's surrounding glaciers. If in any doubt, go with a guide.

To reach **Glaciar Vinciguerra** leave from the gate in Camino del Valle to enter the Andorra Valley and trek the steep ascent through forest paths to **Laguna de los Témpanos**. Follow the right-hand curve around the turquoise lagoon to reach the glacier; you'll need a guide and equipment to negotiate this in winter.

Vinciguerra's ice caves – or any others – should only be visited with a guide. In late 2022, someone died from falling ice at the Jimbo cave.

Glaciar Ojo del Albino is among the most spectacular glaciers – only readily accessible in winter when **Laguna Esmeralda** freezes. Adventurers will need crampons and ice picks.

FROM LEFT: A.PUSHKIN/SHUTTERSTOCK, IMAGEBROKER/ SASHA SELLI-GRABOWSKI/GETTY IMAGES

Fuegian Food & Drink
SPECIALITIES

01 Medialuna
These slightly small croissants are a morning and snack staple. You'll find them either sweet *(de manteca)* or savory *(de grasa)*.

02 Alfajor
Shortbread-like sandwich cookie filled with *dulce de leche* and covered with chocolate or powdered sugar or coconut.

03 Calafate berry
The box-leaved barberry, a native evergreen shrub which flowers yellow each September, has tart berries used in jams and more.

04 Dulce de leche
Silky milk-caramel spread which is often eaten with pastries or added to desserts, and even ice cream.

05 Empanada
Savory pastries you'll find across Argentina, stuffed with beef, ham and cheese, or chicken – the perfect snack.

06 Malbec wine
The most famous Argentinian wines come from Mendoza wine country, a leading malbec region. Chardonnay and torrontés also highly praised.

07 King crab
Centolla (king crab, pronounced sen-*toh*-sha) can grow to 19cm and

live for up to 30 years. They're an Ushuaian speciality.

08 Trout

Trout (*trucha*), like the brown trout of Río Grande, fill rich rivers and lakes throughout the region.

09 Yerba mate

The Argentinian national drink is this loose-leaf tea made from the shrub *Ilex paraguariensis*, native to northeast Argentina.

10 Patagonian lamb

Cordero al palo is lean, tender and grass-fed lamb that is cooked on an open-fire grill.

11 Beef asado

Feast on generous cuts of beef, flame-grilled, at local *parrillas* (grillhouses). *Parrilla* is also the name for the grill itself.

12 Beefsteak mushroom

Keep an eye out in autumn (April and May) for forest-foraged *Fistulina hepatica* and *Fistulina antarctica*, often marinated and tart and tangy.

01 MCRMFOTOS/SHUTTERSTOCK, **02** DOLORES PRECIADO/SHUTTERSTOCK, **03** ILDI PAPP/SHUTTERSTOCK, **04** PATOOUU PATO/SHUTTERSTOCK, **05** XIMENA BRETON/SHUTTERSTOCK, **06** EDSEL QUERINI/GETTY IMAGES, **07** VISUALSTORIES/GETTY IMAGES, **08** GONZALO DE MICEU/SHUTTERSTOCK, **09** ANETA_GU/SHUTTERSTOCK, **10** MAGAIZA/GETTY IMAGES, **11** JEREMY POLAND/GETTY IMAGES, **12** LEWIS PIDOUX/SHUTTERSTOCK

05 RIDING THE Pan-American Highway

NATURE RESERVES | LAKES | SMALL TOWNS

Snaking from Alaska's Prudhoe Bay south across two continents, the Pan-American Hwy becomes Ruta 3 in Buenos Aires, reaching its thrilling finish in Tierra del Fuego. Cruising past Isla Grande's sensational shifting landscapes over 295km is one of the world's iconic road trip finales.

GUSSUSH/GETTY IMAGES

How to

Getting around Roads are well-maintained and easy to navigate.

Río Grande stop Get some driving tips or layover at **Hostel Motorcycle Fin del Mundo** on beachside Ruta 3 (pictured above).

Snacks in Tolhuin Pause for coffee at **Raíces Fueguinas** where number plates line the walls, then grab a treat at **La Unión Panadería**.

Get big views Alight at **Paso Garibaldi** for panoramic views of Lago Escondido and wide blue expanse of Fagnano beyond.

Birdwatch at the reserve

Breathe in the biting sea air and wander among the birds at **Reserva Costa Atlántica**, which stretches 220km along the east coast from Punta Parámo, along Bahía San Sebastián and onwards south of Río Grande to Río Ewan. This reserve is migrating birds' biggest wintering spot on Isla Grande.

01 You've just crossed over from Punta Delgada via Cerro Sombrero in Chile and exited the border at **Bahía San Sebastián**. Head to the windswept beach, the arm of **Punta Páramo** fringing the marine horizon.

02 Career south for an hour and a half to reach **Tolhuin** (pictured), then pass the Selk'nam statue to enter and explore the town center.

03 Stretch your legs around **Lago Fagnano** (pictured) and its nature reserve. Browse the vehicle carcass installations at **Camping Hain**. After around 50km, the snowcapped mountain pass climbs above shimmering **Lago Escondido**.

04 **3005 Moto Cafe** is a Ruta 3 milestone showcasing the stories and vehicles of road trip adventurers including the first person to cross between polar circles by motorbike.

05 Enter Parque Nacional Tierra del Fuego to finish at **Bahía Lapataia** with an obligatory snap at the sign announcing the end of the Ruta. If you started in Alaska you've traveled over 30,000km!

FROM LEFT: LEONARD ZHUKOVSKY/SHUTTERSTOCK, JAVIER GHERSI/GETTY IMAGES

06 A Night on an ESTANCIA

NIGHT SKIES | RURAL FARMS | REMOTE RAMBLES

Much of Tierra del Fuego held extensive sheep ranches known as *estancias*. Today, many have opened to small-scale tourism, offering a unique chance to learn about the region's history and enjoy its magic. **Península Mitre**, a reserve protecting one of Tierra del Fuego's most visually evocative and beautiful terrains, is a land of fairy-tale *estancias*, itinerant wildlife and dramatic seas, skies, shipwrecks and cliffs.

How to

Getting around Drive yourself or coordinate with the *estancia* for a pick-up.

When to go Most *estancia* accommodations are closed during the austral winter (May–October).

Eat on the farms *Estancias* provide meals, though vegetarians should state their food preferences when making reservations.

Get cozy Accommodations range from bunk rooms to historic homes known as *cascos*. Always reserve in advance as communication can be spotty and lodgings are not always receiving guests.

Tierra del Fuego's first estancia Lucas Bridges' autobiography *The Uttermost Part of the Earth* reads like a thriller, depicting the 1870s founding of Ushuaia. His father, Thomas (p48), was the first European colonizing missionary in Tierra del Fuego, and when he rescinded his church role in 1886, Thomas was given the land now called **Estancia Harberton**, lying some 75km from Ushuaia along Ruta J. His descendants still own and run the collection of pastoral red-roofed white buildings where you can visit their museum, restaurants and homestay among islands and pastures flanking the Beagle Channel.

End-of-the-road estancia Along the end of the Ruta J dirt track, around 20km east of Estancia Harberton,

IMAGEBROKER/NORBERT

Best Estancia Day Experiences

Estancia Harberton
Tour **Museo Acatushún**, an impressive array of marine skeletons and fossils, and replica Yaghan huts on nature walks. Reserve a visit to Isla Martillo's penguin colony, then delight in afternoon tea overlooking the channel. The reservation-only restaurant serves Fuegian fine-dining lunches.

Estancia Las Hijas
Welcoming family-run *estancia* with introductions ranging from an hour-long tour to full days.

Estancia El Roble
Every March, this traditional working *estancia* hosts the Fiesta del Ovejura sheepdog festival across its pastures.

Estancia San Pablo
Horseback ride to the **Desdemona shipwreck** and visit the shearing shed.

stands the huge domain of **Estancia Moat**. Established by one of Thomas Bridges' fellow missionaries, it's home to vast swathes of Beagle Channel coastline, fields and rivers. The wild horses and guanaco herds are synonymous with the island's east. It's also the entry point for exploring the Peninsula Punta Mitre's south coast by foot. Join **Alma Calma** (almacalma.net) for a three-day hike from here to **Cabo San Pío**.

The Shipwreck Coast Explore further along Península Mitre where Captain Cook touched Tierra del Fuego in 1769, to discover shipwrecks dotting wide sandy beaches, gauchos ranging and *estancias* slumbering at the end of the world (p42), all in a protected reserve.

Above Marine skeletons, Estancia Harberton

Listings

BEST OF THE REST

Artisanal Chocolate Shops

Chocolates Edelweiss

Amongst Ushuaia's dizzying array of cake and chocolate shops, this tiny, traditional independent gem crafts chocolates that are truly homemade.

La Vieja Aldea

This slick *chocolatería* on Av San Martín purveys chocolate bars, truffles and killer hot chocolate to warm any rainy or snowy day.

Smechén

There are multiple branches of this chocolate shop, so their artisanal, high-end truffle boxes are always near at hand.

Laguna Negra

You can buy myriad chocolates by the kilo, and in addition to superlative sweets – like most of its contemporaries, it doubles as a hot chocolate stop.

Tante Sara

Fuegian patisseries like *chocotortas* and other cakes are so loved that there are now two smart but traditional cafes on Av San Martín and another in Río Grande.

Sweet Treats & Hot Drinks

Ana y Juana

This contemporary Patagonian baker crafts artful South American desserts, feather-light croissants and top coffee drinks in two cheerful branches. Juices, too.

Ramos Generales el Almacén

The feel is Ushuaia circa the Victorian era, so it doubles as a museum with vintage toys, cash registers and treasure chests lining the century-old interiors alongside glass counters displaying decadent desserts.

La Cabaña Casa de Té

You may have to queue for a table at this picture of pastel-hued Patagonian perfection up on the Cerro Martial hillside; an ideal pick-me-up after a walk to the glacier.

Xpresso

Settle into this humming all-day upstairs cafe on Av San Martín for smoothies, baked goods and Beagle Channel views.

El Recreo

This is the place to head for spacious outdoor seating on a fine day...perfect for conversation with coffee or tea alfresco.

Dulces Pau

Small and tucked away on a back street, this is a fun way to get off the beaten track and grab an afternoon snack or caffeine fix.

Sensational Subantarctic Seafood

La Casa de los Mariscos

Look for king crab *(centolla)*, best undressed or gratinated – a regional specialty where the

IMAGEBROKER.COM/ALAMY

La Casa de los Mariscos

crustacean's plump, meaty legs are covered and baked in a ramekin with oozing parmesan cheese.

Volver

For big-occasion dining, intimate Volver is evocatively styled like a fishing hut, fronted by a celebrated chef and famed for its ceviche.

Kaupé

This multiple award-winner wows with its immaculate and imaginative seafood dishes, like *merluza negra* (black hake or toothfish), a delicacy caught by divers in the Beagle Channel.

Kalma Restó

Tuck into Fuegian staples like crab and salmon in a creative context. Black sea bass wears a tart tomato sauce, and summer greens and edible flowers come fresh from the garden. Great wine list, too.

Puerto Almanza

If you have your own wheels, to sample the island's freshest *centolla* make your way down the coast to this port village where the catch of the day fills the seafront restaurants.

Spitfire Grills

La Estancia

For authentic Argentine *asado* (barbecue), it's hard to beat this reliable, well-priced grill. Residents and travelers feast on whole roast lamb, juicy steaks, sizzling ribs and heaping salads.

Bodegón Fueguino

The spot to sample hearty home-style Patagonian fare or gather for wine and appetizers. This century-old Fuegian home is cozied up with sheepskin-clad benches and cedar barrels. A *picada* (shared appetizer plate) for two includes eggplant, lamb brochettes and crab.

FLORORTIZS/SHUTTERSTOCK

Spinach fritters, Bodegón Fueguino

Chez Manu

Heading to Glaciar Martial? Don't miss this quality spot just 2km from town, where you'll feel you're in the middle of nature. Chef Emmanuel adds a French touch to fresh local ingredients, such as Fuegian lamb.

Küar Resto Bar

This chic log-cabin-style seafront hangout offers local beer, cheese boards and tapas, plus ample fresh seafood or Fuegian *cazuelas* (casseroles): a hearty, slow-cooked specialty, an explosion of warming flavors.

Lomitos Martinica

Cheap and cheerful, and full of locals getting takeout, this greasy spoon with grill-side seating serves enormous *milanesa* (breaded meat) or steak sandwiches and offers a good lunch special.

Easy Eats in the Center

Mercado del Jardín

Dip into this affordable food court on Av San Martín where you'll find everything from a sushi truck and fried rice to pizzas.

Isla Vegana

This plant-based bakery located off eastern Av Maipu serves excellent burgers, sandwiches, cakes and salads, and juices, too.

Listings

BEST OF THE REST

Küar 1900

Tapas-like artisanal meat and cheese plates, seafood platters to share and local beers, all in a low-lit ambience. There's more variety at its coastal location.

Food Trucks

Cheap-and-cheerful food trucks fill the plaza in front of Paseo de los Artesanos and the roundabout 1km west on Av Prefectura Naval Argentina.

Craft Beer & Herbed Gin

Patagonia Brewing Co

One of the top spots for a burgeoning collection of micro-brewed craft beer made from glacial water, Patagonian hops and mountain herbs.

Grut '84

You'll find this friendly spot in the center with locally crafted pints paired with burgers and pizza. In Tierra del Fuego beer isn't so much an après-hike thought as an obsession.

La Cabaña Beer Point

Set at the base of Cerro Martial, grab an artisanal beer around the garden fire of this log cabin bar next to a trickling stream.

Jeremy Button Gintonería

This buzzing seafront bar and gin distillery is less unfortunate than its namesake (p48). Whatever your poison, would-be returners should sample a pint or spirit infused with *calafate* – local lore decrees that those who try the Patagonian berry are destined to return.

Torrontes Wine House

If wine and cocktails are more your thing, head to this elegant bar that also serves high-concept, beautifully presented food pairings in its upstairs restaurant.

Remote Península Mitre Estancias

Estancia Maria Luisa

Near the end of the Ruta Complementaria A, and Cabo San Pablo with its equally excellent Estancia San Pablo, this homely guest house has horses for exploring the Península Mitre.

Estancia Las Hijas

Small-scale family visits with horseback riding, sheep mustering and barbecues. Guests stay in basic lodgings with shared bathrooms. Near Estancia Rolito and Estancia San Pablo.

Puesta la Chaira

Part of Estancia Policarpo, this gaucho refuge with ATV adventures is the last manned stay in Península Mitre.

Rancho Ibarra

Near Cabo San Pío, at the southernmost point of Isla Grande, gaucho Luis Andrade welcomes and guides travelers.

HEEBPHOTO/ALAMY

Estancia Rolito

Technical Glacier & Mountain Treks

Monte Olivia

The tallest peak near Ushuaia, at 1326m, can only be scaled in the coldest climes and with help. Its glacier is named after Salesian father Alberto Maria de Agostini, the first person recorded to have climbed Monte Olivia, in 1913.

Cerro Cinco Hermanos

Iconic Cinco Hermanos (1280m) is named after Thomas Bridges' five sons for its jagged five-peaked summit. The trail, 867m up its face, is a challenging 4½-hour round trip.

Alvear Glacier

This ascent is among the area's most ambitious and magnificent to undertake, necessitating overnight camping on the vicinity's third-tallest mountain.

Ice Skating

Laguna del Diablo

This city-center lagoon becomes a vast ice hockey pitch when the water freezes over.

Cerro Castor

Upscale ice-skating in the winter resorts' only ice skating rink. Free entry with a ski pass.

Tachuela Oyarzún Skating Rink

Set on the western waterfront, this outdoor municipal rink is the hub for locals hitting the ice.

Night Views

Auroras

During the austral winter, when sunsets start at 5pm, it's possible to see the Southern Lights emblazoning the subpolar horizon, a psychedelic light show of green and pink auroras dancing across the skies.

HENRIQUE NISHIMURA/SHUTTERSTOCK

Lago Escondido

Dogsledding

Whizz through the snow-covered forests of the Tierra Mayor Valley by dogsled.

Spa Soak

Revel in the contrast of cold air and thermal waters over panoramic views via alfresco hydrotherapy during a night visit to the spa of the resort Arakur.

Stargazing

Stargaze at dazzling subantarctic constellations on the beach and nature reserve of Playa Larga.

Hike & Dine

Take a guided night hike and ski lesson on Cerro Martial then dine in a forest dome with Patagon Mountain Agency.

Starlit Waters

Join a tour from Ushuaia to Lago Escondido for a sunset kayak beneath the stars and *cordillera* (mountain range).

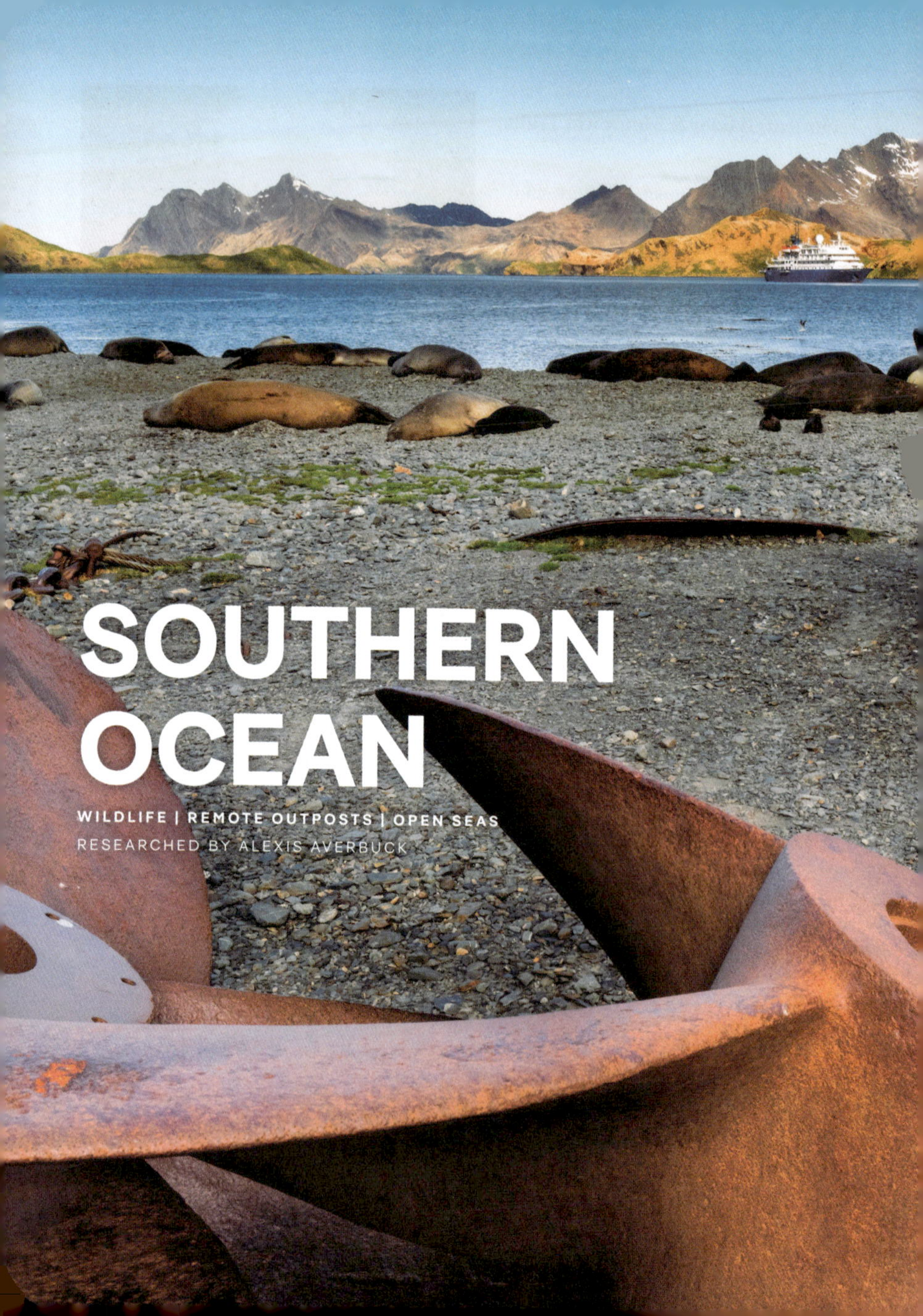

SOUTHERN OCEAN

WILDLIFE | REMOTE OUTPOSTS | OPEN SEAS

RESEARCHED BY ALEXIS AVERBUCK

SOUTHERN OCEAN

Trip Builder

The rarefied southern reaches of the Atlantic, Indian and Pacific Oceans form the fifth ocean of the world, the Southern Ocean. Its wild waters surround Antarctica and isolate it geographically, biologically and climatically, and its islands are abundant havens for breeding wildlife.

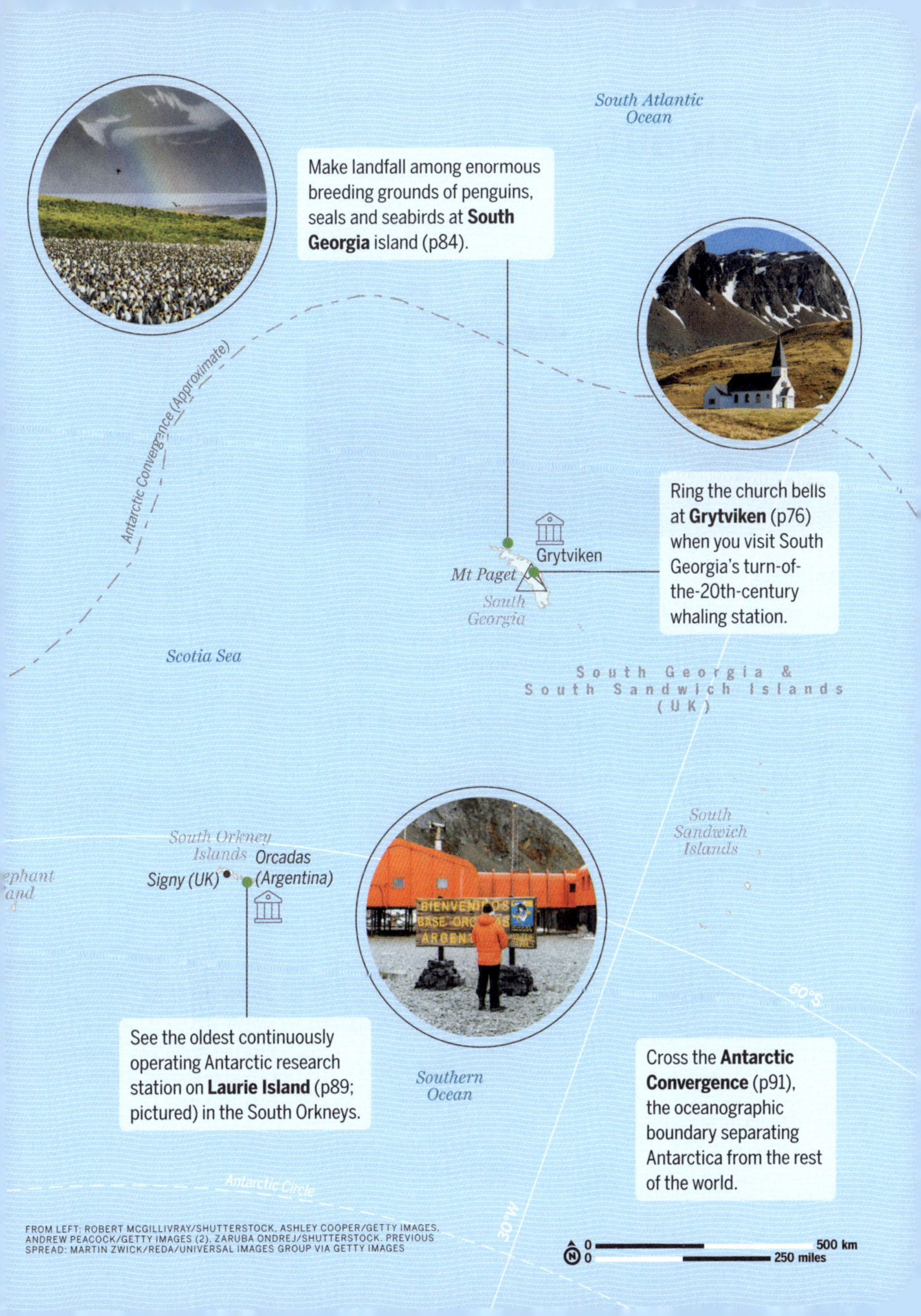

Make landfall among enormous breeding grounds of penguins, seals and seabirds at **South Georgia** island (p84).

Ring the church bells at **Grytviken** (p76) when you visit South Georgia's turn-of-the-20th-century whaling station.

See the oldest continuously operating Antarctic research station on **Laurie Island** (p89; pictured) in the South Orkneys.

Cross the **Antarctic Convergence** (p91), the oceanographic boundary separating Antarctica from the rest of the world.

FROM LEFT: ROBERT MCGILLIVRAY/SHUTTERSTOCK, ASHLEY COOPER/GETTY IMAGES, ANDREW PEACOCK/GETTY IMAGES (2), ZARUBA ONDREJ/SHUTTERSTOCK. PREVIOUS SPREAD: MARTIN ZWICK/REDA/UNIVERSAL IMAGES GROUP VIA GETTY IMAGES

Practicalities

DURKTALSMA/GETTY IMAGES

ARRIVING

Cruise Most visitors to Antarctica arrive by cruise, which, depending on your itinerary, will take you to peri-Antarctic Islands en route. Adding the Falkand Islands (Islas Malvinas) and South Georgia add time, but are worth the detour.

Fly It's possible to fly into the Falkland Islands (on LATAM from Chile) or King George Island (pictured above) in the South Shetland Islands.

Fly-cruise With fly-cruise options you fly into King George, then switch to a ship to cruise south.

FALKLANDS CLIMATE

The islands' climate is temperate.

It has frequent high winds.

Maximum temperatures rarely reach 24°C (75°F).

Even on the coldest winter days the temperature usually rises above freezing.

HOW MUCH FOR A

Pint of craft beer in Stanley £3.40

Falklands fly-along-seat by internal airplane £55–85

Guided Falklands kayak outing £100

SHOW NO FEAR

Keep well clear of fur seals. But if they run at you, wave your arms, look large and yell at them to back off.

SOUTH GEORGIA ENTRY & EXIT FORMALITIES

Visitors to South Georgia must apply for an entry permit online (eta.entry.gov.gs) at least two weeks before entering. There is a fee of £200 and you must prove health insurance that includes evacuation. Cruise and tour companies usually prompt passengers to apply for the permit or apply for a group permit for all on board.

Yachts also must submit a Vessel Booking Notification to the Government of South Georgia and the South Sandwich Islands and pay separate harbor fees.

TOP: WOLFGANG KAEHLER/ALAMY

FALKLANDS ORIENTATION

About 40% of Falklanders are native born, some tracing their ancestry back six or more generations. Today more than 80% of the 3662 Falklanders (sometimes called 'Kelpers') live in Stanley, and about 1200 British military live at Mt Pleasant base. The rest of the islanders live in 'Camp,' the name given to all of the Falklands outside Stanley.

TOP ONLINE RESOURCES

Website	Coverage
falklandislands.com	Central source on the Falkland Islands (Islas Malvinas).
falklandsconservation.com	Landscape and marine conservation and wildlife info in the Falklands.
fitv.co.fk	Falkland Islands Television for news and current events.
gov.gs	South Georgia & South Sandwich official site with loads of information, including permit requirements.
sght.org	South Georgia Heritage Trust, the primary history and wildlife conservation group.

MONEY

The Falkland Islands (Islas Malvinas) and the shop in Grytviken, South Georgia use GBP (£) and cards, though the official currency in the Falklands is the Falkland Islands Pound (FKP), which is valueless outside of the islands.

07 Stanley LIFE

CRAFT BEER | DEEP HISTORY | VILLAGE STROLLS

The capital of the Falkland Islands (Islas Malvinas), Stanley, is little more than a village. Despite rapid growth since 1982, the old part of town retains its charm, with corrugated iron walls and colorful roofs. Flower-bedecked gardens and patriotic flags add to the vivid colors, which contrast with the surrounding moorlands. Old pubs are reminders that some Falkland traditions remain unchanged.

ANDREW PEACOCK/GETTY IMAGES

How to

Get around Stanley's picturesque and compact layout makes it an excellent place to explore on foot.

Stay over If you have the chance to overnight, Stanley has several hotels, B&Bs and guest-houses.

More info The **Jetty Visitor Centre** (falklandislands.com) on the quay is packed with maps of walks and other info (or download their app).

LIGHTROCKET VIA GETTY IMAGES

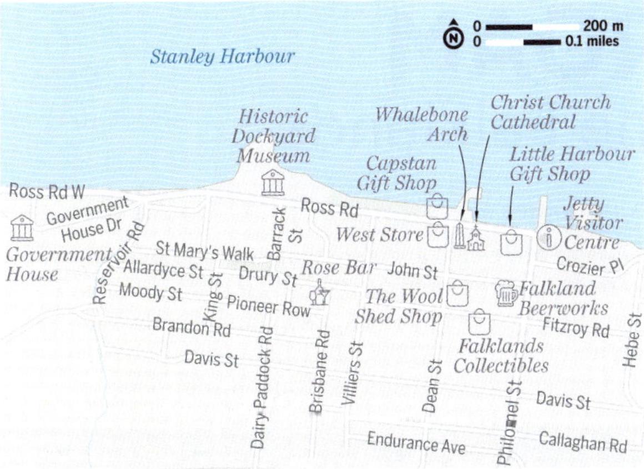

Above left Stanley waterfront
Below left Christ Church Cathedral

Historic curiosities Spend an hour immersing in the memorabilia at the waterfront **Historic Dockyard Museum** (falklands-museum.com), which is crammed with fascinating artifacts from everyday life on the islands, testimonials about the 1982 war, natural-history specimens and fine displays about shipwrecks. The Reclus Hut used in Antarctica in the 1950s is here, too. Outbuildings include a printing office and **Falklands Collectibles**, where garrulous Phil sells stamps and currency. Or simply get a drink in the cafe and watch seabirds soar.

Photo ops Perhaps Stanley's most photographed landmark, rambling **Government House** has been home to London-appointed governors since 1845 and was briefly occupied by the Argentine commander during the 1982 occupation. The 1892 **Christ Church Cathedral**, with its brightly painted, corrugated-metal roof and attractive stained-glass windows, is the town's most distinguished landmark. The **Whalebone Arch** out front is pic-worthy, too, as are the old shipwrecks along the waterfront.

Hunt for cool souvenirs This is a prime chance to stock up on local arts and crafts, woolly hats, penguin T-shirts and the like. Jam-packed **Little Harbour Gift Shop** and **Capstan Gift Shop** each have a great selection of postcards, books and locally produced gear like woolen wear and craftwork, as does the **Jetty Visitor Centre**. Knitters should make a beeline to **The Wool Shed Shop** for Falkland fibers. The big grocery **West Store** is your spot if you want British snacks like Hobnobs.

Pub Life

Stanley's pubs offer a unique opportunity to experience Falkland flavor, hospitality and culture. We run the **Falkland Beerworks**, the world's most remote craft brewery. Stop by, say hello and enjoy a pint (or two) of our fresh, locally brewed traditional craft beers. We also serve the famous local gin, wines, ciders and non-alcoholic beverages. You could make it part of a pub crawl, and continue on to **Groovy's**, **Victory Bar**, **Globe Tavern**, **Deano's Bar** and **UnWined**, all within a block, then pop over to the **Rose Bar**.

Tara Francis *is brewer and co-owner at Falkland Beerworks in Stanley. falklandbeerworks.com*

08 ROAM the Falklands

SEABIRDS | BEACHES | INLAND TRAMPS

The Falkland Islands (Islas Malvinas) are a popular addition to many Antarctic voyages, and they're well worth seeing in their own right for their spectacular penguin, seal and albatross populations. Two main islands, East Falkland and West Falkland, and more than 700 smaller ones cover 12,173 sq km rich with wildlife and myriad walks and excursions – strap on your boots!

NATHALIE MICHEL/GETTY IMAGES

How to

Getting around The Falklands are laced with 400km of roads, but many are rough tracks. You'll fly (p213) to the furthest reaches, hire a car from a taxi (ask at the **tourist office**) and ferry between East and West Falkland.

Stay in the countryside Some remote parts of 'Camp' offer serene getaways, like **Sea Lion Lodge**.

Arrange a tour Outfitters include **Falklands Outdoors** (falklandsoutdoors.com) with hikes, kayaking, mountain biking and more.

DAVID CHAPMAN/ALAMY

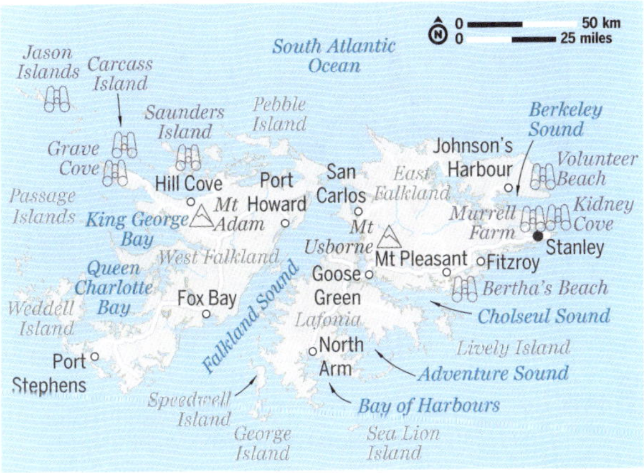

Penguins and seabirds Besides the five types of penguin (gentoo, king, macaroni, Magellanic and rockhopper) that breed here, you'll discover many equally interesting and uncommon birds. To begin, head to **Murrell Farm** (kidneycovetours.com) where four of the penguin species congregate. **Kidney Cove** will wow you with its swirls of soft, rose-colored sands and turquoise waters. **Volunteer Beach** is popular for its enormous king penguin colony. South of Stanley, **Bertha's Beach** is gentoo central.

Fly west to **Saunders Island** – home to gentoo, king, rockhopper and Magellanic penguins – and **Grave Cove**, for gentoos, and if you're lucky, dolphins. **Carcass Island** has never had cats, rats or mice, so small birds are abundant. The island takes its name from HMS *Carcass*, which, along with HMS *Jason*, established Port Egmont on Saunders Island in 1766–67. From here, you can take a boat out to the remote **Jason Islands** for the largest colony of black-browed albatross in the world. Plus over 100,000 pairs of rockhopper penguins.

Flora Among the 13 endemic plants you'll see on walks – get walking maps at the **tourist office** or download their app – are several unusual species, including snake plant *(Nassauvia serpens)*, with its long stalks and tiny leaves, and Felton's flower *(Calandrinia feltonii)*, a caramel-scented, magenta-blossomed annual until recently thought to be extinct in the wild.

Vanilla daisy *(Leuceria suaveolens)*, while not endemic, is still interesting – its flowers smell remarkably like chocolate.

Above left Gentoo penguins, Grave Cove **Below left** Vanilla daisy

Get the Lay of the Land

East Falkland has the islands' most extensive road network, with a highway to **Mt Pleasant** base and airport and **Goose Green** village. Once you're out of Stanley things get quiet. The northern part of the island is rolling and often mountainous. It's joined by an isthmus to Lafonia in the south, which is flat and dotted with lakes.

Port Howard is West Falkland's oldest farm, dating to 1866. Gorgeous headlands around **Port Stephens** are open to the blustery South Atlantic. Thousands of rockhopper penguins, cormorants and other seabirds breed here.

The only native land mammal, the Falkland Island wolf (or warrah), is extinct.

Who Was Ernest Shackleton?

THE EXPLORER WHO DEFINED ENDURANCE

The name Shackleton is synonymous with adventure, bravery and Antarctic survival. A fascination for visitors to the Ice, business schools studying leadership and lovers of good swashbuckling stories alike, his journey of hardship and heroism is a highlight from the Heroic Age of Antarctic Exploration.

Left *Nimrod* expedition **Centre** Ernest Shackleton **Right** *Endurance* expedition

HULTON ARCHIVE/GETTY IMAGES

Anglo-Irishman Ernest Henry Shackleton (1874–1922), second of 10 children, lived by his family motto: *Fortitudine vincimus* (By fortitude we conquer). An indefatigable worker with a charming, forceful personality, Shackleton was badly stung by his own ill-health during Scott's 1902 *Discovery* expedition (p144). Back in Scotland, Shackleton worked as a PR man for a Glasgow steelworks. Its owner, William Beardmore, took a shine to Shackleton and sponsored his next Antarctic expedition.

The Nimrod Expedition

The British Antarctic Expedition sailed from New Zealand in *Nimrod*. When Shackleton arrived at the Ross Ice Shelf in January 1908, he built his hut at Cape Royds (p144) on Ross Island, before pushing for the Pole. Thwarted by diminished supplies, Shackleton and his men were forced to abandon their attempt only 180km from their goal.

The Endurance Expedition

Shackleton regrouped, setting his sights on crossing Antarctica. The Imperial Trans-Antarctic Expedition would sail *Endurance* to the Weddell Sea coast, establish a base, and trek across the continent via the Pole. At the top of Beardmore Glacier, the crossing party would be met by another group, which would have landed at Ross Island (p134), sailing *Aurora* from Hobart.

Endurance sailed from Plymouth on August 8, 1914, calling at South Georgia before pushing into Weddell Sea pack ice. Soon it was squeezing through ever-narrower leads. By January 19, 1915, *Endurance* was caught.

LEFT & RIGHT: FRANK HURLEY/SCOTT POLAR RESEARCH INSTITUTE, UNIVERSITY OF

The incredible events that followed have grown to legend, and much of it was caught on film by expedition photographer Frank Hurley. The ship, inexorably crushed by grinding ice floes, finally sank on November 21. Shackleton and his men lived on the pack ice for five months before sailing three open lifeboats to **Elephant Island** through freezing waters. Since the island was little more than a windswept rock, Shackleton and five others navigated another 1300km across open sea to seek help from whalers at South Georgia. After 16 exhausting days, they landed there, completing one of history's greatest navigational feats. Frank Worsley used a sextant in deep cloud cover amid 15m waves.

Shackleton on South Georgia

Unfortunately, their South Georgian landfall was at **King Haakon Bay**, on the uninhabited southwest coast; the whaling stations were on the island's northeastern side. Shackleton, Worsley and Tom Crean crossed the island's 1800m mountain range and ice crevasses – the first recorded instance of this being done. After 36 hours they neared **Stromness** but impassable ice cliffs forced them to descend an icy, 9m waterfall. When they arrived at the station on May 20, 1916, their long beards, matted hair and ragged clothes caused the first three people they met to flee.

A ship was sent to rescue the three men at King Haakon Bay. After three failed attempts over four months, the 22 men at Elephant Island were also rescued. Everyone on *Endurance* had survived.

Shackleton mounted a final journey to the Antarctic, the *Quest* expedition. Upon reaching **Grytviken**, South Georgia, he died of a heart attack on January 5, 1922 aboard his ship; he is buried at Grytviken (p77).

Live Donkey

On the *Nimrod* expedition, Shackleton, with Eric Marshall, Jameson Adams and Frank Wild, pioneered the route up to the Polar Plateau via the Beardmore Glacier, named for the expedition's patron. The decision to turn back was the hardest of Shackleton's life. He told his wife, Emily, later: 'I thought you'd rather have a live donkey than a dead lion.'

Still, they had achieved a remarkable run, beating Scott's furthest south by 589km, discovering almost 800km of new mountain range, and showing the way to anyone attempting the Pole after them.

09 The Whalers of GRYTVIKEN

WHALING | MUSEUM | GRAVES

Grytviken is South Georgia's only whaling station that can be visited; hazardous material and dangerous structures mean the others are off-limits. The spacious harbor contains not only the cemetery where Ernest Shackleton and Frank Wild are buried, but a fascinating walk through whaling history and a museum and gift shop.

ZARUBA ONDREJ/SHUTTERSTOCK

How to

BYO everything There are no visitor accommodations on South Georgia. Travelers sleep and eat on board their ships and yachts.

Write home Buy and write postcards at the museum shop – they sell postage and will mail them for you.

Dive into history
Heritage trusts, like the South Georgia Heritage Trust (sght.org) and the Antarctic Heritage Trust (nzaht.org) are repositories of Antarctic stories and memorabilia that work to educate, preserve and conserve.

N CHOLAS_DALE/GETTY IMAGES

Shackleton at Grytviken

Ernest Shackleton's name is inextricably linked with South Georgia, and visits to the island often include landings at places associated with his expeditions. **Grytviken** is the most important and most visited. Shackleton first stopped here in November 1914 on his way south with *Endurance*. From the whalers he learned that it was a bad ice year in the Weddell Sea. Although he delayed his departure by several weeks, the ice got his ship nevertheless. The manager's house in **Stromness** where he first arrived on foot is undergoing preservation using heritage Norwegian building techniques.

Shackleton returned to Grytviken in 1922. This time southbound on the *Quest*, he died of a heart attack aboard his ship, moored alongside the whaling station, early on the morning

RICHARD I'ANSON/GETTY IMAGES

Ring My Bell

Don't miss the restored 1913 Norwegian **Whalers' Church**, near the football pitch. Grytviken's first pastor, Kristen Löken, lamented: 'religious life among the whalers left much to be desired.' Inside are memorials to Grytviken's founder, Carl Anton Larsen, and to Shackleton, whose funeral was here. Go upstairs to ring the two bells.

Above left Grytviken's abandoned whaling station **Left** Rusted chain at whaling station **Above** Harpoon gun

of January 5. A few hours before, he wrote his final diary entry: 'In the darkening twilight I saw a lone star hover, gem like above the bay.'

Whalers' Cemetery

Today, Shackleton's grave in the Grytviken **Whalers' Cemetery** is one of South Georgia's highlights for many visitors, along with the Memorial Cross erected by his *Quest* shipmates in 1922 at Hope Point, across King Edward Bay from the cemetery. On the back of the granite headstone (engraved with the nine-pointed star that Shackleton used as a personal emblem) is one of his favorite quotations, from poet Robert Browning: 'I hold that a man should strive to the uttermost for his life's set prize.'

In November 2011, Frank Wild's ashes were buried alongside Shackleton's after a ceremony in the church attended by Shackleton's and Wild's descendants. Wild was Shackleton's 'right-hand man.'

South Georgia Museum & Shop

When entering this wonderful museum, be sure to look up to see the wandering albatross mounted overhead. The museum occupies the former Norwegian station manager's house, built in 1916. It's filled with fascinating exhibits on South Georgia's wildlife and history, objects from the whaling station, like whalers' handicrafts and the cinema projector, and amazingly, Worsley's original almanac with which he navigated to South Georgia (p75). A replica of the boat, the *James Caird*, is on display, too. The shop sells clothing, books, souvenirs and Shackleton whisky (p145) and the staff is very knowledgable about South Georgia.

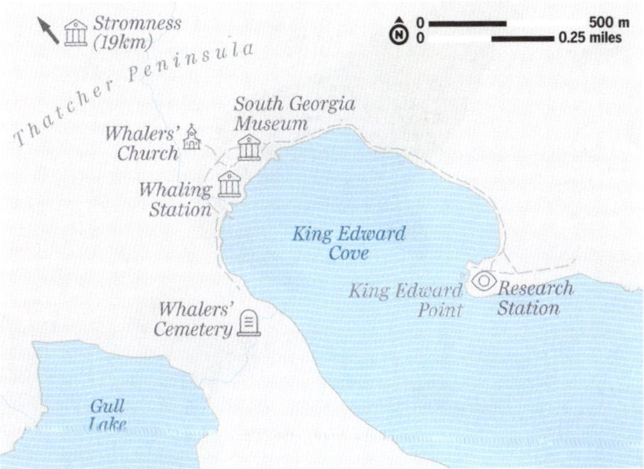

Left South Georgia Museum and Shop **Below** Ernest Shackleton's grave, Whaler's cemetery

The 63 other graves include 19th-century sealers, Norwegian whalers and one Argentine soldier killed during the Falklands War.

Whaling Station

Grytviken, South Georgia's first and longest-running station, operated from 1904 to 1965. Although a whole whale could be butchered in as little as 20 minutes, it was sometimes hard to keep pace with the catcher boats. As many as four dozen whales might be brought in at once, with the whole of Grytviken Bay covered by carcasses, which were inflated with compressed air to keep them afloat. Working overtime to keep up meant double pay.

Wander the station's enormous blubber vats and flensing plan...if you're lucky, the staff at the museum will be offering one of their excellent tours, which will describe how the factory worked.

The tour usually ends at the weathered steel sculpture – including original rivets – by Michael Visocchi called *Commensalis: The Spirit Tables of South Georgia*. It commemorates the 175,250 whales killed at the island between 1904 and 1966.

Cetaceans & SEALS

01 Antarctic fur seal
The smallest seal, it's related to sea lions and dogs. Hunted to near-extinction in the 19th century, they have since rebounded.

02 Weddell seal
Placid, permanent dwellers of the Antarctic, Weddells are the world's southernmost mammal. They keep holes in the ice open for diving.

03 Southern elephant seal
Named for the males' giant proboscis, this largest of seals lumbers on land but is graceful at sea, diving 2km and submerging for two hours.

04 Leopard seal
Built for speed, this long, sleek predator has a giant maw that opens to reveal supersharp canines and molars.

05 Crabeater seal
This krill-eating seal doesn't eat crab, but dwells year-round in the pack-ice zone, and has the largest population of all seals.

06 Humpback whale
Very active at the ocean's surface,

humpbacks weigh 34,000kg and breach while slapping their enormous flippers, which reach one third of their body length.

07 Orca

Born into a pod of up to 50 related dolphins (not whales!) orca travel up to 55km/h, hunt together and have their own 'dialect' of calls.

08 Sei whale

Part of the rorqual group of baleen whales, seis are the third-largest whales in the Southern Ocean.

09 Minke whale

The most abundant baleen whales in the Southern Ocean. Small, fast swimmers, minkes often approach slow-moving vessels.

10 Fin whale

Adult fin whales reach speeds of 37km/h and may not feed in winter, relying on their accumulated blubber.

11 Blue whale

The largest animal that has ever lived. About 5000–8000 exist in the Southern Hemisphere, having been hunted to near-extinction.

The Rise & Impact of Antarctic Sealing & Whaling

ANTARCTICA'S FIRST HUMANS ON THE HUNT

Sealers were among the first to explore the Antarctic waters, discovering islands, naming regions and slaughtering seals until the end of the 19th century. Whalers came next, bringing their industry near the beginning of the 20th century, with most whale species being hunted to near extinction in an area that is now protected.

Left James Weddell's brig, *Jane* **Centre** Nathaniel Palmer **Right** Old whaling station, Deception Island

DEA PICTURE LIBRARY/GETTY IMAGES

The Sealers

During the sealing era (about 1780 to 1892), more than 1100 sealing ships visited Antarctic regions, compared to barely 25 exploration ships. The sealers were motivated by profit, not discovery, though a few firms, notably Enderby Brothers of London, spent vast sums on exploration.

Nearly a third of the peri-Antarctic islands were discovered by sealers. These hunters, however, considered their finds top secret and kept the information to themselves (although drunken sailors were known to boast about newfound sealing grounds).

Sealing was an extremely hard life. Gangs were typically dropped off on a promising beach and left for months at a time while the ship continued in search of other sealing grounds. The sealers lived in tents, rude huts or small caves among the rocks. The brutality of the seal-killing itself impressed even the sealers.

Sealers' Discoveries

Among the most intrepid sealers was American Nathaniel Palmer (1799–1877), son of a shipyard owner. He went to sea at 14, and on his second sealing voyage to the South Shetlands in 1820, Palmer anchored inside the caldera of Deception Island (p100), almost certainly the first to do so. He spotted Trinity Island (p105) and probably the Antarctic Peninsula. In 1821, he sailed south as far as Marguerite Bay (p117).

Similarly, Scotsman James Weddell (1787–1834), an upholsterer's son, discovered the South Orkney Islands, which had just been sighted by Palmer and George Powell. In 1823, he collected six skins of a new seal species – now

SMITH ARCHIVE/ALAMY

WOLFGANG KAEHLER/ LIGHTROCKET VIA GETTY IMAGES

known as the Weddell. He sailed south into a sea normally covered in impenetrable ice, getting 344km further than Cook. He named the sea for King George IV but the name was later changed to honor Weddell.

From Whaling to Conservation

Antarctic whaling was established in 1904, with 183 whales killed. By 1912–13, six land stations, 21 factory ships and 62 catcher boats killed and processed 10,760 whales. South Georgia was an important early catching ground. By the 1920s, advancing technology (particularly the stern slipway, which allowed the entire whale to be winched aboard a floating factory ship for processing) shifted work to pelagic, or open-ocean, whaling. Since they were at sea, pelagic factory ships avoided government limits on whale-hunting. Deception Island had both land and sea operations.

By 1930–31 the annual kill had increased to 40,000. Except for during WWII, whaling continued at this level for the next 20 years. As each species was driven to near extinction, whalers switched to a new species.

The International Whaling Commission (IWC; iwc.int) was established in 1946 to regulate the orderly development of the whaling industry worldwide. It agreed to a moratorium, which came into force in 1986, on all commercial catches. Nowadays, the IWC moratorium has come under pressure from whaling nations such as Japan and Norway.

In 1994 the IWC established the Southern Ocean Whaling Sanctuary to protect the whales' primary feeding grounds and encourage depleted species to recover. There's no commercial whaling, even if the worldwide moratorium were to be lifted. There is an exception for whaling for scientific purposes.

Historic Catches

Historically, whale oil was used for lighting, lubrication and tanning; in the early years, it was mainly a Norwegian and British industry. For an idea of the numbers of whales caught, we can look to records from South Georgia, the main site of land-based operations. From 1904 to 1965, when whaling at South Georgia ceased, a total of 41,515 blue whales were caught, along with 87,555 fins, 26,754 humpbacks, 15,128 seis and 3716 sperm whales.

If you visit the Grytviken whaling station (p76) you'll see the new memorial to the whales killed.

10 South Georgia's WILDLIFE

SEALS | PENGUINS | SEABIRDS

The many fjords and bays of South Georgia's northeastern coast are lined with fantastic wildlife-breeding beaches. Thanks to the high mountains, this coast is protected from prevailing westerlies, which is why animals and historic whaling stations cluster here.

ANDREW PEACOCK/GETTY IMAGES

How to

Know your mountains The Allardyce Range forms the island's spine of sharp, heavily glaciated peaks. The highest point is **Mt Paget** (2934m), first ascended in 1964.

See the ice Glaciers cover 57% of the 3755-sq-km island.

Find baby seals Elephant seals and fur seals breed and pup in November and December.

ANDREW PEACOCK/GETTY IMAGES

YONGYUT KUMSRI/SHUTTERSTOCK

Abundant & Varied Wildlife Breeding Grounds

Salisbury Plain is the stuff of an adventurer's dream. This huge, flat expanse of green spreading out in front of Grace Glacier chirps with over 250,000 king penguins when they converge during molting season, making it South Georgia's second-largest king rookery. Climb the tussock-covered hillside to enjoy wonderful views, not only of the rookery but also of the island-studded bay. Elephant and fur seals also haul out on these beaches to breed, give birth and molt.

Where is the largest king-penguin rookery, you may ask? **St Andrews Bay** where as many as 300,000 raucous, smelly kings congregate on 3km of gravel and black-sand beach. This is also South Georgia's largest elephant-seal

Miraculous Southern Elephant Seal

Those gallumphing elephant seals have huge reservoirs of blood (22% of their body mass) and can slow their hearts to just a single beat per minute. The deepest dive recorded is an amazing 1930m. They can stay down for two hours, and rest for surprisingly short intervals at the surface.

Above left King penguins, Salisbury Plain **Left** South Georgia pintail (p86) **Above** Light-mantled sooty albatross (p86)

breeding beach, where normally 6000 cows haul out at the height of the season. But their populations have been badly hit by avian flu. You can carefully cross two glacial rivers (the three glaciers behind the beach are all in significant retreat) to hike up a rise overlooking the magnificent rookery.

Joining exceptional wildlife with fabulous scenery, **Gold Harbour** has 25,000 breeding pairs of king penguins, interspersed with several hundred pairs of gentoos, all up near the glacier face. You'll also find Antarctic terns, southern giant petrels and beautiful light-mantled sooty albatross.

Last but not least, **Cooper Bay**, named for Cook's first lieutenant during his 1775 visit, hops with over 20,000 chinstrap penguins, the island's largest colony. They're joined by thousands of macaroni and gentoo penguins, and several hundred pairs of kings.

Species to Spot

South Georgia pipit
The world's most southerly songbird, whose sweet chirps contrast with the rugged landscape.

South Georgia pintail
This unassuming little duck eats meat.

Southern elephant seal
Their gargantuan size, particularly highlighted when males fight, displays the sheer power of nature.

Hybrid burnet
You can only find the natural cross of lesser and greater burnet in South Georgia.

Antarctic fur seal
Breeding season plays out in dramatic style along the island's beaches.

Will Wood, *the On-Island Operations Manager of South Georgia Museum, which is run by South Georgia Heritage Trust. @southgeorgiaheritagetrust*

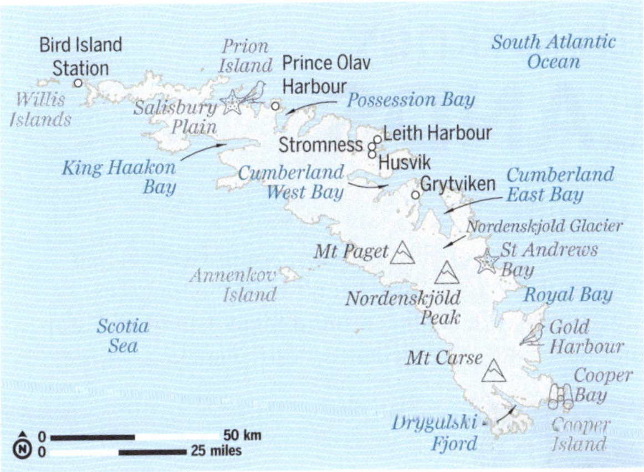

Left Southern elephant seal
Below South Georgia pipit

FROM LEFT: DENNIS STOGSDILL/SHUTTERSTOCK, ANDREW PEACOCK/GETTY IMAGES

Rats, Reindeers & Other Non-Native Species

It's taken over 20 years of work and £10 million, but the eradication of non-native mammals – namely rodents and about 6750 reindeer, the latter introduced by whalers in 1911 – was finally accomplished in 2018. Sami herders and Norwegian marksmen were called in to cull the reindeer, and the meat was sold in the Falkland Islands. The program used helicopters to drop bait for the rodents in even the most isolated spots.

As a result, the wild birds have rebounded, but alas now face avian flu (p227). Your ship will encounter strict biosecurity (p227) in South Georgia. Just like the rest of the Antarctic, authorities fight to keep non-native species out – even as small as a sesame seed on a strip of jacket velcro – so that local flora and fauna flourish, unhindered.

Islet Life

Prion Island is home to magnificent wandering albatross and thousands of burrowing seabirds, which thrive there since the island never had any of the destructive rodents introduced to South Georgia by early visitors. Four other historically rat-free islands (Cooper, Annenkov, Albatross and Bird) also harbor enormous seabird populations, but they are off-limits to tourist landings.

11 South Orkney ISLANDS

HISTORIC BASE | GLACIERS | WILDLIFE

Few ships visit the South Orkney Islands, between South Georgia and the Peninsula, but they're a treat. Land on Laurie Island with the longest continuously operating Antarctic base, or Zodiac around Signy Island and stop into Shingle Cove on Coronation Island for excellent wildlife-viewing.

ANDREW PEACOCK/GETTY IMAGES

How to

Stay warm Layer up! The South Orkneys are 85% glaciated and the weather is cold, windy (westerlies) and overcast. On average the sun shines less than two hours a day.

Get even further The group also includes the aptly named Inaccessible Islands (29km west) – if you visit, you will be in the rare few; only about 1000 people visit the South Orkneys every year.

LAURA HEDIEN/GETTY IMAGES

ASHLEY COOPER/GETTY IMAGES

Clockwise from bottom left Fur seal; Cemetery, Orcadas Station; Orcadas Station

Antarctica's oldest base In 1903 Scottish explorer William Speirs Bruce wintered on mountainous **Laurie Island**, where he helped set up a meteorological station. When you go, look for the ruins of his stone hut, Omond House, at the end of the beach. When Bruce left in 1904 the station was turned over to Argentina, which has operated it ever since, making it the oldest continuously run research facility in Antarctica.

The base was renamed **Orcadas Station** (dna.gov.ar) in 1951. You'll get to tour its three-room museum in the 1905 **Casa Moneta**, which features a replica of an early hut, as well as artifacts, some from Bruce's expedition. Chinstraps, Adélies and gentoos nest nearby. Also visit the small cemetery where the earliest grave dates from 1903.

The wildlife of Signy Island The captain who took the first whale in the area, Petter Sørlle, named Signy Island after his wife in 1912. *Tioga*, the first ship to undertake open-ocean whaling in Antarctica, wrecked at Signy in 1913. A Norwegian shore station opened on in 1920 and further processed *skrotts* (stripped carcasses) cast off by floating factories. Now there's a tiny summer-only **research base**.

Nowadays, tourists don't land at Signy, but can Zodiac around observing fur seals; chinstrap, Adélie and gentoo penguins; southern giant petrels and South Georgia shags.

Whale Hotspot Under Threat

Few places on Earth concentrate marine life like the South Orkneys. Humpbacks and fin whales gather in extraordinary numbers – possibly the planet's highest whale density – drawn by explosive krill blooms fueling the whole Southern Ocean ecosystem (p90).

Yet these same waters host the world's most intense krill fishery. Industrial vessels harvest krill at a rate of 100 to 400 whales-worth per ship. A proposed CCAMLR Marine Protected Area would change that calculus, but geopolitics keeps it stalled.

Coming here feels urgent. You're witnessing something both magnificent and precarious.

Dr Ted Cheeseman, *whale biologist and co-founder of Happywhale, with 23 seasons in Antarctica.*

Currents of Cold, Bountiful Life

THE RICH, WILD SOUTHERN OCEAN

Crossing the Southern Ocean is the price you pay – or reward you receive – in reaching Antarctica by ship. Undulating blue waves thrive with the ever-popular penguins and whales people come to see, and a rich ecosystem that supports the world's food chain. This is the ocean that dictates the Earth's weather patterns.

Left Drake Passage **Centre** Antarctic krill **Right** Antarctic cod or toothfish

BOBBUSHPHOTO/GETTY IMAGES

Drake Passage

More than 90% of Antarctic cruises visiting the Antarctic Peninsula sail from Ushuaia, Argentina, and cross the Drake Passage – 1000km of ocean between South America and Antarctica. No landmasses impede low-pressure systems circling Antarctica, so westerly winds reach great speeds and seas can get very rough. The crossing generally takes two days. Smooth seas are known as the 'Drake Lake,' their opposite is called the 'Drake Shake,' also referred to as 'paying the Drake Tax.' Once your ship reaches the South Shetlands or the Peninsula, nearly all uncomfortable motion ceases.

Antarctic Krill

One of the most essential creatures in these waters is the Antarctic krill *(Euphausia superba)*. It's a 6cm-long planktonic crustacean that swarms south of the Antarctic Convergence. An even smaller species is ice krill *(Euphausia crystallarophias)*. Krill is sifted out of the water by baleen whales, and eaten by many seabirds (especially penguins), squid, fish and crabeater seals. Without krill, the ecosystem of the Southern Ocean would collapse.

Fisheries target Antarctic krill (p193) and quotas are now set by Commission for the Conservation of Antarctic Marine Living Resources (CCAMLR).

You might ask, what do krill eat? Phytoplankton or algae. These in turn contain chlorophyll and take up carbon from carbon dioxide dissolved in the water. When plankton dies it takes the carbon down into the sediments. This has prompted research on how much carbon can be taken

GERALD CORSI/GETTY IMAGES

CAVAN IMAGES/ALAMY

out of the atmosphere by phytoplankton to help combat climate change.

Fish & Benthic Species

The Southern Ocean supports more than 270 species of fish and the nutrient-rich area just north of the Antarctic Circumpolar Current gives rise to some of the world's most productive fisheries. Scientists study fascinating species such as the Antarctic cod or toothfish *(Dissostichus mawsoni)*, which survive in subzero waters without freezing because of 'antifreeze' proteins in their blood. They grow to 2m and 135kg. Their hearts beat only once every six seconds.

Members of the ice fish family Channichthyidae, such as the mackerel ice fish *(Champsocephalus gunnari)*, have no hemoglobin and are 'white-blooded.' Oxygen is carried in their blood plasma, but this has only 10% of the oxygen-carrying capacity of fish blood containing hemoglobin. To make up for this, ice fish have more blood, a larger heart, larger blood vessels and more gill surface area, and can even exchange oxygen through their tails.

All Antarctic fish grow slowly, with most coastal species requiring five to seven years before they can breed. This is of great importance when deciding sustainable catch limits.

The communities that inhabit the seafloor around Antarctica are called the benthos, and are as rich in plants and animals as a tropical coral reef. They comprise Antarctica's true indigenous flora and fauna, adapted to life in a cold ocean over tens of millions of years (such as Turquet's octopus, *Pareledone turqueti*). Nearly every time a deep-sea sample is brought up, it includes many species new to science.

Antarctic Convergence

On your way to Antarctica you'll pass over the Antarctic Convergence, also known as the Antarctic Polar Front. The ocean south of the convergence differs greatly in salinity, density and temperature. North of this seasonally and longitudinally varying line, the summer surface seawater temperature is about 7.8°C (46°F), while south it's 3.9°C (39°F). During winter it's approximately 2.8°C (37°F) in the north and 1.1°C (34°F) south. A great mixing occurs at the Convergence, and nutrients from the seafloor are brought to the surface, making it a highly productive area for algae, krill and other small creatures at the base of the Antarctic food web.

ANTARCTIC PENINSULA

PENGUINS | WHALES | ICE FORMATIONS

RESEARCHED BY ALEXIS AVERBUCK

ANTARCTIC PENINSULA
Trip Builder

The most accessible and warmest part of the continent, the beautiful Antarctic Peninsula, extends a welcoming arm north toward Tierra del Fuego. This dramatic landscape of snow-covered peaks and iceberg-studded channels weaving through countless islands is also Antarctica's primary breeding ground for seabirds, seals and penguins.

Photograph eye-popping scenery and ice in **Paradise Harbor** (p107), Lemaire Channel and Charlotte Bay.

Send a postcard from a UK base-turned-museum at **Port Lockroy** (p113).

Sail south of the Antarctic Circle along the route of Jean-Baptiste Charcot to **Marguerite Bay** (p117).

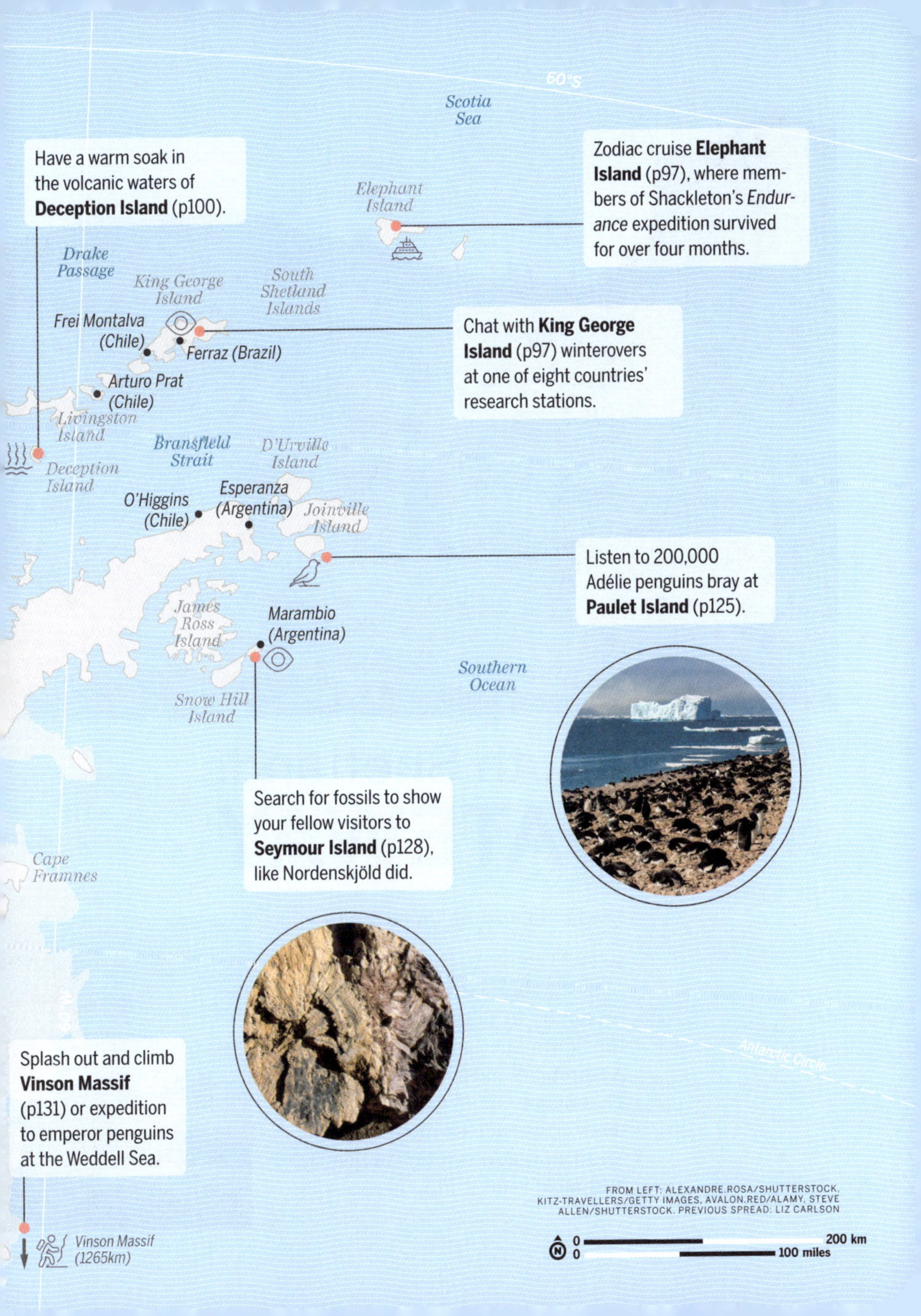

Have a warm soak in the volcanic waters of **Deception Island** (p100).

Zodiac cruise **Elephant Island** (p97), where members of Shackleton's *Endurance* expedition survived for over four months.

Chat with **King George Island** (p97) winterovers at one of eight countries' research stations.

Listen to 200,000 Adélie penguins bray at **Paulet Island** (p125).

Search for fossils to show your fellow visitors to **Seymour Island** (p128), like Nordenskjöld did.

Splash out and climb **Vinson Massif** (p131) or expedition to emperor penguins at the Weddell Sea.

FROM LEFT: ALEXANDRE.ROSA/SHUTTERSTOCK, KITZ-TRAVELLERS/GETTY IMAGES, AVALON.RED/ALAMY, STEVE ALLEN/SHUTTERSTOCK. PREVIOUS SPREAD: LIZ CARLSON

12

South Shetlands GATEWAY

BASES | PENGUINS | ARTIFACTS

Thanks to their spectacular scenery, abundant wildlife and proximity to Tierra del Fuego, the South Shetlands are one of Antarctica's most visited areas. This major island group is half a day's cruise across the Bransfield Strait to the Antarctic Peninsula, and most cruises stop here.

ISADORA ROMERO/BLOOMBERG VIA GETTY IMAGES

How to

Fly in Fly-cruise packages fly from Punta Arenas, Chile to **Teniente Rodolfo Marsh Martin Airport** on King George Island.

Overnight ashore Frei Station has facilities for tourists who fly in and stay overnight. Check with your tour company; many go straight onto a cruise ship.

Climb a crater Off King George Island, at **Penguin Island** climb the red volcanic cone (170m; Deacon Peak) for great views of the crater and chinstrap penguins.

LWOLFARTIST/WIKIMEDIA/CC BY 2.0

Join the Crowds at King George Island

King George Island is the largest of the South Shetlands and the first stop in the Antarctic for many tourists. Less than 10% of the island's 1295 sq km is ice-free, yet it supports over 10 bases connected by more than 20km of tracks because it's so accessible from South America.

You'll likely land on the island's southern coast at **Turret Point**, named for a group of prominent rock stacks above the beach, on the eastern end of **King George Bay**. It's a nesting area for Antarctic terns, chinstrap and Adélie penguins, blue-eyed shags and southern giant petrels.

ASHLEY COOPER PICS/ALAMY

Wash Ashore on Elephant Island

At the South Shetlands' northeastern end, **Elephant Island** was named 'Sea Elephant

Sealers & Gentoos of Greenwich Island

As early as 1820, circular **Yankee Harbor**, on **Greenwich Island**, was an important anchorage for sealers. A gravel spit makes it a favorite yacht anchorage today. On the spit, look for an old sealer's try-pot. Further up the beach, by the Argentine *refugio* (refuge) built in the 1950s, visit the gentoo penguin rookery.

Above left King George Island **Below left** Teniente Rodolfo Marsh Martin airport, King George Island **Above** Gentoo penguins, Greenwich Island

Island' by the British sealers in the early 1820s. It was here that 22 members of Ernest Shackleton's 1915 *Endurance* expedition (p74) spent 135 days.

At **Point Wild**, on the northern coast, where the men lived beneath two upturned boats, you'll find a bust of Luis Pardo, commander of the *Yelcho*, who rescued them on August 30, 1916. Landings are difficult; heavy surf often prevents even Zodiac tours. Fur seals and chinstrap penguins dot the shore.

At **Cape Lookout**, a 240m-high bluff on the southern coast, visit chinstrap, gentoo and macaroni penguins.

Elephant Island is also home to 2000-year-old moss colonies and peat nearly 3m deep.

Penguins on Livingston Island

Livingston Island was the first land sighted in the Antarctic when William Smith saw it in February 1819. The island's prominent 1700m central peak, Mt Friesland, is often obscured

Antarctica's First Tourists

The first Antarctic tourist flight, by LAN Chile in 1956, flew over the South Shetlands and the Antarctic Peninsula.

Two of the earliest cruises to Antarctica, by the Argentine ship *Les Eclaireurs*, reached the South Shetlands in January and February 1958.

In 1959 the Argentine ship *Yapeyú* and the Chilean vessel *Navarino* both took passengers to the South Shetlands.

In 1972 the *Lindblad Explorer*, the first passenger ship built specifically for polar cruising, ran aground in King George Island's Admiralty Bay. The 90 passengers were rescued by a Chilean naval vessel, and a German tugboat towed the ship off the rocks 18 days later.

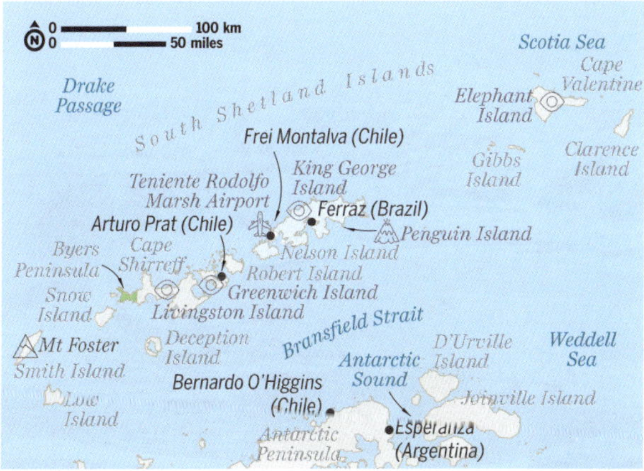

Left Heading towards Point Wild, Elephant Island **Below** Whale skeleton, Walker Bay beach

by cloud; it was first climbed in 1992 by a pair of Spaniards.

The island was a major early-19th-century sealing center, and the remains of shelters and artifacts have been found on many beaches. The entire Byers Peninsula on the island's western end is protected, because it contains the greatest concentration of 19th-century historical sites in Antarctica.

Hannah Point, on the south coast, is an extremely popular stop, with its large chinstrap and gentoo rookeries and the occasional macaroni pair nesting among them. The point is named after British sealer *Hannah*, wrecked on Chistmas 1820, and an extremely popular stop with its large chinstrap and gentoo rookeries and the occasional macaroni pair nesting among them. Be careful of southern giant petrels nesting: they're skittish and will abandon eggs or chicks if nervous.

On a hill above the Hannah Point landing beach, a prominent red vein of jasper runs through the rock. From this lookout you can survey a sheltered beach on the opposite side of the point where elephant seals bask and young male fur seals spar.

Walker Bay is occasionally used as a landing site with its fascinating collection of fossils left by researchers on a table-like rock among a group of boulders. There are also seal jaws and teeth, and penguin skulls and skeletons.

FROM LEFT: TIM BIEBER/GETTY IMAGES, HOLGER LEUE/GETTY IMAGES

13 VOLCANIC
Deception Island

VOLCANO | HOT SOAK | CHINSTRAPS

Unique among the South Shetlands is Deception Island, a beautiful 'restless' volcano. Easily recognized on any map by its broken-ring shape, Deception Island's collapsed volcanic cone provides one of the safest natural harbors in the world, despite periodic eruptions.

EVENFH/SHUTTERSTOCK

How to

Into the crater To reach this enclosed harbor, ships navigate a tricky 230m-wide break in the volcano's walls, known since early-19th-century sealing days as **Neptune's Bellows** for the gales that blow through.

Avoiding shipwreck Boats have to steer clear of Ravn Rock (named by Charcot in 1908), just 2.5m beneath the channel's surface.

Territorial challenges Argentina, Chile and Britain all make claims to Deception, with its superb location and harbor.

ROBERTHARDING/ALAMY

Sailing into Deception

As you enter Deception Island's harbor, notice the striking colors of the rock faces. Watch for pintado petrels nesting on cliffs on the starboard side. On the port side, at **Entrance Point** lies the wreck of British whale-catcher *Southern Hunter*, which ran aground on New Year's Eve in 1957 while avoiding an Argentine naval vessel steaming in. The British yelled for help, but the Argentines assumed they were shouting and waving as part of the New Year's celebrations and continued past.

ROBERT MCGILLIVRAY/SHUTTERSTOCK

What's a 'Restless' Volcano?

The volcano that formed Deception is classified as 'a restless caldera with a significant volcanic risk.' A violent explosion 10,000 years ago blew about 30 cu km of molten rock from the island, and the volcano's summit

Antarctic Volcanoes

Beneath icy Antarctica, plate tectonic forces are at work. In places the continent is slowly rifting apart, much like East Africa. You'll find active volcanoes in the western Ross Sea, including best-known Mt Erebus (p146), West Antarctica and along the Peninsula. Polar Earth Observing Network (polenet.org) monitors seismic sensors around Antarctica.

Above left Telefon Bay (p102) **Below left** Chinstrap penguins, Baily Head (p103) **Above** Hot springs, Pendulum Cove (p103)

collapsed to form the caldera, now flooded. In 1923, water in this interior sea called **Port Foster** boiled and stripped the paint from ships' hulls. In 1930 the floor of the harbor dropped 3m during an earthquake. You won't find much marine life in this volatile zone.

Two 1967 eruptions forced the evacuation of the Argentine, British and Chilean research stations, and the Chilean station was destroyed. In 1969, five station members escaped a hail of volcanic bombs and falling cinders by carrying pieces of corrugated iron over their heads. Continued volcanic events keep Spanish scientists *(ign.es)* monitoring seismic activity year-round.

Telefon Bay is a spectacular place to view the results of volcanic activity, with scree and ash hills and craters.

Steamy Landings

Inside the caldera, you may land at **Whalers Bay** on a black-sand beach cloaked in

Whaling Station

In 1906 a Norwegian-Chilean whaling company began using Whalers Bay for its floating factory ship, the first of several. In 1912, a shore station opened to process the meat and bones (which contain 60% of a whale's oil) of 3000 whale carcasses that the ships had abandoned after stripping them of their blubber. By 1912–13, 12 floating factories, 27 catcher boats and the shore station processed more than 5000 whales (p82).

Today, several wooden huts stand disintegrating. Flensing boats (factory ships for removing blubber) and water barges lie buried to their gunwales in black volcanic sand. Huge boilers and tanks now stand rusting under the southern sky.

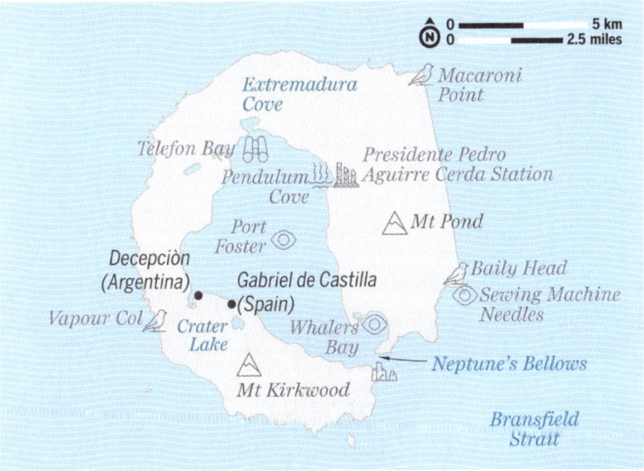

Left Whaling station remains, Whalers Bay **Below** Pintado petrel (p101)

mysterious white clouds of sulfur-scented steam. Dig your boots into the sand to find heat escaping from subterranean volcanic vents. The island's sloping, snow-covered walls reach 580m above the beach.

At **Pendulum Cove**, named for experiments performed by British naval captain Henry Foster in 1829, you can experience one of Antarctica's rarest activities: go for a hot dip. A geothermally heated stream trickles into the bay and you'll find a small area where scalding and frigid waters mix – ideal for a few people to soak in comfort. The off-limits ruins of Chile's destroyed **Presidente Pedro Aguirre Cerda Station** are behind the beach. When walking, be careful not to squash unique mosses and lichens.

Largest Chinstrap Rookeries

Chinstraps are Deception's most common penguins, with several rookeries exceeding 50,000 pairs each. You'll find them on the southwestern coast at **Vapour Col** and on the northeastern coast at **Macaroni Point**. **Baily Head** (also called Rancho Point), home of perhaps the largest chinstrap rookery on the Peninsula, is a natural amphitheater with a melt stream running through it. Just south, look out for sea stacks called the **Sewing Machine Needles**.

14 Frozen Passages & HARBORS

ICEBERGS | SCENERY | WHALES

Most cruises make a beeline for at least one of the spectacular, iceberg- and wildlife-rich coves and bays along the central Peninsula. Snap great photos, record dramatic video of icebergs calving, and spy on penguins, seabirds, seals and whales in their natural habitat.

CHARLES H. JONES PHD/SHUTTERSTOCK

How to

Cruise a canyon

Sailing from the South Shetland Islands towards the Peninsula, you'll pass **Trinity Island** with its penguin rookery in **Mikkelsen Harbor**. Offshore, at **Spert Island**, Zodiac through the basalt and andesite canyons, sea arches and rock tunnels.

Take to the sea

Pre-book a kayaking expedition if it's offered with your cruise – it's incredible to quietly maneuver around these shining waters and icebergs.

HOLGER LEUE/GETTY IMAGES

Wildlife Cruising Through Ice Palaces

Count yourself blessed if you Zodiac cruise **Cierva Cove**, one of the first magnificent inlets on the Antarctic Peninsula as you sail south. The Breguet and Gregory glaciers calve, and ice cliffs line its northern side, guaranteeing a parade of ice formations, brash ice and glittering icebergs. It's also the breeding ground for 10 bird species (eg gentoos, chinstraps, shags and terns). Weddell, crabeater and leopard seals laze about, and humpback and minke whales visit frequently. Spot tiny Argentine **Primavera Station** here, too.

PAUL A. SOUDERS/GETTY IMAGES

The Ladies' Bays

Charlotte Bay, filled with recently calved icebergs, is one of the Peninsula's most exquisite spots. If you land at its entrance, **Portal Point**, look for the foundations of the British

De Gerlache's Beset Expedition

The 1897 *Belgica* expedition of Adrien de Gerlache 1897 left Antwerp with a crew including Norwegian first mate Roald Amundsen. They mapped Gerlache Strait and its islands before a 377-day imprisonment in pack ice. Darkness and scurvy toyed with the men's sanity. Read the tale in *Madhouse at the End of the Earth* (2021) by Julian Sancton.

Above left Wilhelmina Bay (p106)
Below left Minke whale, Booth Island (p107)
Above Zodiac cruise, Cierva Cove

Antarctic Survey hut, now relocated to the Historic Dockyard Museum (p71) in Stanley. On the southern side of the Reclus Peninsula, **Wilhelmina Bay** offers an alternative for cruising and kayaking among humpback whales feeding on krill swarms, while several glaciers descend to the sea.

Islands in the Stream

Motor into **Errera Channel**, where Zodiac cruising in the ice-choked channels can be spectacular, and you're greeted by three islands. The littlest, half-dome-shaped **Cuverville Island** is popular for one of Antarctica's largest gentoo penguin colonies. Snow algae stains the slopes lined with deep moss beds, which shouldn't be stepped on.

On **Danco Island**, named for the De Gerlache expedition's geophysicist, Émile Danco, who died in the Antarctic, gentoos nest right up to the summit of a 180m peak. **Rongé Island**, the largest, is home to several large colonies of gentoos and chinstraps.

The Drama of Charlotte Bay

Portal Point is my favorite place in Antarctica, where light drifts across towering icebergs and whales gather to feed. The place carries a quiet romance, as breath merges with wind and ice. In such remoteness, every sound matters: the thunder of calving ice, the slow roll of melting giants under warming skies. Here, the ocean teaches humility. Wildlife sharpens the senses, silence calms the heart, and reflection comes easily. The panoramic beauty feels authentic and profound. Once it enters you, it never truly leaves.

Wayne Broomfield, *a polar guide who lives for the wild, shares his wisdom and traditions. @inuitphotographer*

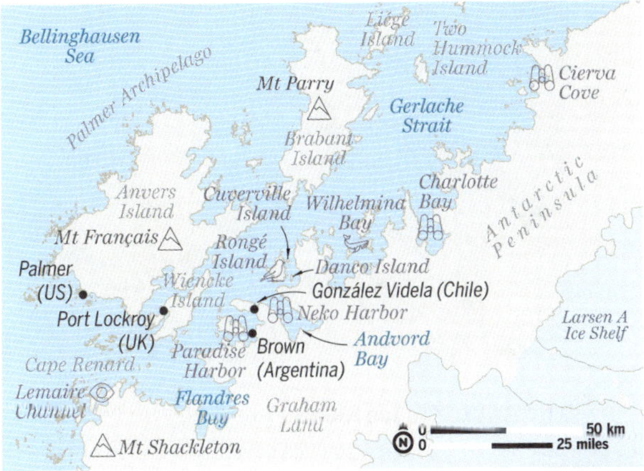

Left Charlotte Bay (p105) **Below** Copper deposits, Paradise Harbor

The Stars of the Central Peninsula

Neko Harbor is named for Norwegian whaling ship *Neko*, which operated here between 1911 and 1924. The glacier calves with a thunderous roar, offering dramatic video footage. Hundreds of gentoos nest on the hillside. As you gaze over the iceberg-filled waters, recall American long-distance swimmer Lynne Cox, who in December 2002 swam nearly 2km (in 25 minutes) in the 0.5°C (33°F) waters here – fatal for almost anyone else. Read about it in her memoir *Swimming to Antarctica* (2004).

Even the hardened early 20th-century whalers recognized the extreme splendor when they named **Paradise Harbor**, with its majestic icebergs and reflections of the surrounding mountains in the water. It's a favorite place for Zodiac cruising around the ice calved from the glacier at the head of the bay. You'll pass blue-eyed shags nesting on cliffs colored blue-green by copper deposits, emerald green by moss, and orange by lichens.

Spectacular, steep-sided **Lemaire Channel** runs 11km between the mountains of **Booth Island** and the Peninsula. The passageway is deep – mostly over 140m – and at just 1600m wide it's only visible once you're almost inside. Ice sometimes blocks the way, so ships may be forced to retreat and sail around Booth Island.

The Thinning White Frontier

STUDYING ANTARCTICA'S ICE IS CRITICAL TO UNDERSTANDING CLIMATE CHANGE

With climate change melting its vast ice sheets, Antarctica – despite its remoteness – sits at the forefront of climate research. Discoveries of the impacts on the ice and ecosystems hit international media regularly, as does news of sea-level rises and myriad inter-related global systems that affect us all.

Left Tabular iceberg (p155) **Centre** Adélie penguins on ice floe **Right** Melting iceberg, Lemaire Channel (p107)

MARIO TAMA/GETTY IMAGES

The Antarctic Ice Sheet

Satellite images show that ice covers 99.82% of Antarctica. The Antarctic ice sheet has an area of about 13.3 million sq km (1.7 times the size of Australia). This ice is up to 4776m thick in some locations and on average is about 2200m thick – giving it a total ice volume of about 28 million cu kilometers. In some places its gargantuan weight has depressed the underlying landmass by nearly 1600m.

This enormous amount of ice has formed through the accumulation of snow over millions of years, and exists in a state of dynamic equilibrium. The amount of snow deposited in any one year is relatively very low – Antarctica is a desert and the driest continent on Earth. Because the snow has been deposited over so many years without melting, the ice sheet provides a natural archive that glaciologists and climatologists study for evidence of past environments (p168) and of climatic changes.

Ice Shelves & Icebergs

The Antarctic ice sheet is the 'iceberg factory' of the Southern Ocean. Due to pressure created by its own weight, the ice flows from the high interior toward the Antarctic coast, becoming ice shelves (floating but attached to shore), then large slabs break off to form icebergs. The total volume of ice calved from the ice sheet each year is about 2300 cu km, and it has been estimated that there are about 300,000 icebergs in the Southern Ocean at any one time. Individual icebergs range in dimension from a few meters (often called 'growlers') to about 5m ('bergy bits') to over 100km long.

COPYRIGHT JEFF MILLER/GETTY IMAGES

PAUL SOUDERS/GETTY IMAGES

These larger icebergs are tabular in shape (p155) and form by calving from the large Antarctic ice shelves (eg Ross, Filchner or Amery). Typically, they're about 30m to 40m high (above sea level) and over 300m deep. At any one time four or five gigantic icebergs may be afloat in the Southern Ocean, such as A-23a, which measured over 1000 sq km (p156). In 2000, one of the world's biggest icebergs – about the size of Connecticut – broke free from the Ross Ice Shelf (p158). It held enough fresh water to supply the world for over a year.

The Big Melt

Antarctica's ice sheets contain 90% of the world's ice, holding about 70% of the world's fresh water. If they melted, it is estimated the world's oceans would rise by more than 58m. When Antarctica's ice shelves are lost along the continent's edges, continental ice moves more rapidly toward the sea. Studies show that a major contributor to this loss is warming ocean temperatures, which undermine ice shelves from subsurface cavities. Additionally, increasing winds are predicted to increase ocean upwelling rates, which would also increase subglacial melting. Such events interlock with other complex systems (such as ice formation and ocean salinity and acidity), and there's a major push to better monitor and analyze these changes.

Right now the West Antarctic Ice Sheet (WAIS) is losing mass and is Antarctica's greatest contributor to sea-level rise. One 2023 study predicts the melting is currently irreversible in the 21st century.

Ice thickness is measured using radar and GPS positions of markers in the ice sheet, which over time reveal the speed of the ice flow. The European Space Agency (esa.int) uses the satellite CryoSat to measure Antarctica's ice sheet.

Western Peninsula & Climate Change

The western Peninsula is one of the most rapidly warming places on Earth. The average wintertime temperature in the Palmer area has risen over 6°C (43°F) in the past 50 years. This has resulted in receding glaciers and decreased winter sea ice. As weather warms, chinstrap and gentoo penguins are increasing in number, while the more cold-loving Adélies are decreasing (85% since 1974). By 2060, 30% of Adélie colonies are expected to be in decline, and by 2099, that number is predicted to be 60%. Palmer Station Long Term Ecological Research (pallter.marine.rutgers.edu) studies the region's changes. Read more in *The Ferocious Summer* (2008) by Meredith Hooper.

15 Postcards from THE STATION

BASES | WHALES | POST OFFICE

Palmer Station and Port Lockroy feature pioneering science and preserved polar history. Anvers Island and its Patagonia Bay captivate with abundant wildlife and dramatic landscapes offering unforgettable encounters at the edge of the world. Write a postcard home while penguins dive offshore.

JUAN BARRETO/AFP VIA GETTY IMAGES

How to

Britain's Antarctic start In 1944, a secret British naval operation, unofficially called 'Operation Tabarin' (for a bawdy Parisian nightclub) established Base A at Port Lockroy, the nation's first overwintering station. It was staffed until 1962 but then fell into disrepair.

Mailing a postcard At Port Lockroy, both buy your postcard and pop it in the mail using GBP, US dollars, euros or credit cards.

GREGORY "SLOBIRDR" SMITH/ WIKIMEDIA/CC BY-SA 2.0

The Whales of Patagonia Bay

Mountainous **Anvers Island**, 70km long, was discovered by De Gerlache in 1898 and named for the Belgian province of the same name. The truly lucky will sail into its **Patagonia Bay**, one of several vast inlets carving its eastern shore. Zodiac cruising here will bring you next to the pffff-ing vents of humpback whales, feeding in tandem.

SERGEJ ONYSHKO/SHUTTERSTOCK

Science in Action at Palmer Station

Palmer Station was built in 1968 on the island's southwest coast and named to honor American sealer Nathaniel B Palmer, who in 1820 was one of the first to see Antarctica. Palmer accommodates 44 people in summer but only about 25 people 'winter over.' Research focuses on long-term monitoring of the marine ecosystem (mainly seabirds

Base Life

Small bases are often staffed only by scientists, while large ones, like McMurdo (p168), have a bustling crew of support staff, from hairdressers to heavy-equipment operators. Scientists may come for just the few weeks of their observations. You'll usually find a lively sense of camaraderie and social life.

Above left View from Palmer Station, Anvers Island **Below left** Palmer Station **Above** Humpback whale

and krill), atmospheric studies and the effects of climate change. While the station is accessible by sea year-round, only 12 cruise ship visits are permitted annually to avoid disruption to research. Tourists get a walking tour, including an interesting peek into two aquariums filled with anemones, mollusks, sea urchins, krill and fish. You may also shop at the station store (which accepts credit cards and US dollars).

Adélie Rookery at Torgersen Island

The Adélie rookery just offshore at **Torgersen Island** is often visited in tandem with Palmer Station. Since 1974, however, the Adélie population here has dropped by 60% to fewer than 3300 pairs, due to climate-induced changes in sea ice. At Litchfield Island, just west of Torgersen, the Adélies are already gone after 15,000 pairs nested there for at least 600 years.

The Bahía Paraíso Wreck

Antarctica's worst environmental disaster occurred on January 28, 1989, when the 131m Argentine naval supply ship *Bahía Paraíso*, with 234 passengers and crew (including 81 tourists), ran into a submerged rock pinnacle off DeLaca Island, 3km from Palmer station. The pinnacle ripped a 10m gash in the ship's hull, spilling 645,000L of diesel fuel and other petroleum products and creating a slick that covered 30 sq km. No one was injured. Palmer residents towed the *Bahía Paraíso*'s unmotorized lifeboats to shore and fed the passengers and crew. Two nearby cruise ships and an Argentine vessel carried everyone out of Antarctica.

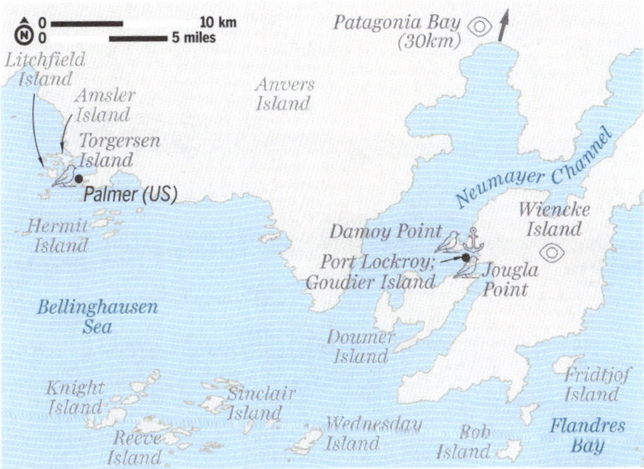

Left Post office, Port Lockroy
Below Food supply stock, Goudier Island museum

Hit the Post Office at Port Lockroy

De Gerlache (p105) named **Wiencke Island** for Carl August Wiencke, a young seaman who fell overboard and drowned while trying to clear *Belgica*'s scuppers.

You'll find one of the most popular tourist stops in Antarctica in the 800m-long harbor on the west coast of Wiencke: **Port Lockroy**. This is thanks to **Base A**, the former British station-turned-museum on tiny **Goudier Island**, operated by the UK Antarctic Heritage Trust (ukaht.org). You can buy postcards and mail them from here (£2 to £3 postage)...a unique chance.

Until about 1931 Port Lockroy was a major whaling harbor. Around the landing site, you can spot chains and eyebolts and the date '1921' inscribed in the rock; these were moorings for *Solstreif*, one of 11 factory ships that processed whales here.

Visits are usually made in conjunction with landings at the gentoo rookery at nearby **Jougla Point**, where other highlights include blue-eyed shags and a composite whale skeleton reconstructed on the shore.

Your ship may stop at **Damoy Point**, too, for its gentoo rookery and historic Argentine and British huts.

FROM LEFT: GODDARD_PHOTOGRAPHY/GETTY IMAGES; MARTIN HARVEY/GETTY IMAGES

16 SOUTH OF the Antarctic Circle

HISTORY | WILDLIFE | REMOTE BASES

Few cruise ships make it south of the Antarctic Circle, but if you do, you'll be rewarded with vast, deserted stretches of glaciated sea coast, interesting historic stations and two active bases, along a route first charted by famed explorer Jean-Baptiste Charcot.

THE_CROFTER/GETTY IMAGES

How to

Research in the far south The UK's **Rothera Research Station**, with its 900m gravel airstrip, holds up to 160 people. Argentina's **San Martín Station**, the most southerly year-round Peninsula station, on **Barry Island**, is home to 20.

Breaking the ice Ponant's (ponant.com) *Le Commandant Charcot* hybrid electric icebreaker goes where others can't: emperor penguins in the Weddell Sea, Marguerite Bay and 31 days across the continent, from Ushuaia to Tasmania.

Three Penguin Populations

Y-shaped **Booth Island** – discovered by a German whaling and sealing expedition in 1873–74 – forms the western side of the Lemaire Channel (p107). Its highest point is 980m Wandel Peak, and it's one of very few places in the Peninsula where you'll be able to see three species of penguin (Adélie, gentoo and chinstrap) nesting alongside one another – most of the others are off-limits to tourism. Charcot's French Antarctic Expedition aboard *Français* spent the winter of 1904 at **Port Charcot** (the explorer named it for his famous physician father) on Booth's northwest end. A cairn, pillar and plaque from the expedition are protected as a historic site.

If you sail along the west coast of Booth, you'll pass **Pléneau Island** home to

Above left Marguerite Bay (p117)
Below left Snow algae, Petermann Island (p116)

thousands of gentoos and rich banks of pink and green snow algae.

Algae, Penguins & History

Home to the world's southernmost gentoo colony, 135m-high **Petermann Island**, at 65°10' S, is one of the most southerly landings most cruises make. Just under 2km, the island was discovered by the same 1873–74 German expedition. Adélies, gentoos and blue-eyed shags nest here, and look for abundant snow algae.

Charcot wintered aboard *Pourquoi Pas?* at **Port Circumcision**, a cove on the island's southeast coast, where they set up a shore station, with huts for meteorological, seismic, magnetic and tidal research. They had discovered it on New Year's Day 1909 and named it for the Feast of the Circumcision (January 1), when Christ was circumcised. You can still spot a cairn on **Megalestris Hill** and a 1955 Argentine refuge hut. Near the hut, a cross commemorates three British Antarctic Survey

Pourquoi Pas? Charcot's Last Voyages

In 1908, Charcot again sailed south in the *Pourquoi Pas?* (Why Not?), which carried the name he had christened his toy boats with as a child. The group continued their survey work on the western Peninsula, discovering the Fallières Coast, circling Adelaide Island and finding Marguerite Bay. The ship had electric lighting and a 1500-volume library, invaluable during the winter of 1909, when they were icebound at Petermann Island.

Twenty-six years later, Charcot and *Pourquoi Pas?* were again sailing treacherous waters, this time off Iceland, when a gale arose and claimed captain, ship and all but one of the 43-man crew.

Charcot's First Expedition

French physician Jean-Baptiste Charcot (1867–1936) used his inheritance of 400,000 gold francs and a Fragonard painting, *Le Pacha*, to build schooner, *Français*, and outfit it with lab equipment. With it, in 1904 he took the French Antarctic Expedition down the west coast, wintering on Booth Island. When Charcot returned home, his wife Jeanne divorced him.

OLEKSANDR MATSIBURA/SHUTTERSTOCK

(BAS) men who died in 1982 attempting to cross the sea ice to Faraday Station (now Ukraine's **Akademik Vernadsky Station**).

Sailing south, keep your eyes out for the **Yalour Islands**, 2.5km in extent, where about 8000 pairs of Adélies nest among beautiful examples of orange lichens and green mosses, as well as small clumps of Antarctic hairgrass.

Ghost Towns & Wildlife in Marguerite Bay

Charcot reached gigantic, glacier-lined **Marguerite Bay** on his 1909 expedition and named it for his second wife. The **Dion Islands** at the northern end of the bay was once home to the only emperor penguin rookery in the western Peninsula region, but it's disappeared due to climate change. Nearby, **Pourquoi Pas Island** is home to Adélies, and sometimes visited by orca deep in the pack ice.

Further south along the bay's coast and named for the home port of Connecticut sealer Nathaniel Palmer (who reached the region in 1821), **Stonington Island** is an Antarctic ghost town. Two abandoned stations, about 200m apart, are rarely seen by tourists, being so far south.

FROM LEFT: NANCY PAUWELS/SHUTTERSTOCK, LBM1948/WIKIMEDIA/ CC BY-SA 4.0

Left Cross commemorating three BAS men, Petermann Island
Top right Akademik Vernadsky Station
Bottom right Orange lichen, Yalour Islands

Penguins & SEABIRDS

01 Macaroni penguin
The world's most abundant penguin, distinguished by their orange-plumed 'eye-brows' and black chins.

02 Adélie penguin
This small tuxedo-ed penguin masses in main-land Antarctica breeding colonies, ranging 600km north in winter.

03 Emperor penguin
Antarctica's giant is known for winter breed-ing, deep diving and amazing survival skills.

04 Chinstrap penguin
Named for the thin black band under its head, chinstraps 'toboggan' on their belly.

05 King penguin
Smaller than emperors, the king penguin breeds in large colonies close to the shore.

06 Gentoo penguin
The black-and-white gen-too is distinguished from the slightly smaller Adélie and chinstrap penguins by its orange bill.

07 Antarctic shag or cormorant
Inshore-feeding birds, cormorants' presence alongside a ship are a sure sign of approaching land.

08 Sooty shearwater
Found circumpolar at sea, they breed on islands off New Zealand and Cape Horn.

09 Wandering albatross
Their genus name *Diomedea* commemorates Trojan hero Diomedes, whose companions were turned into large, white birds by the Greek gods.

10 Antarctic tern
The Peninsula is home to Antarctic terns, and at sea you'll see Arctic terns, long-distance migrants from the northern hemisphere.

11 Gray-headed albatross
Breeding biennially, these endangered birds can fly 12,000km around the Southern Ocean during off-years.

12 South polar skua
The South Polar skua – a scavenger and an aggressive hunter – is the world's most southerly bird.

13 Northern giant petrel
These seabirds come to land only to breed, and myriad species circle the skies of the Southern Ocean.

01 ZARUBA ONDREJ/SHUTTERSTOCK, **02** SADIE WHITELOCKS/SHUTTERSTOCK, **03** VLADSILVER/SHUTTERSTOCK, **04** ANTON_IVANOV/SHUTTERSTOCK, **05** ERIC ISSELEE/SHUTTERSTOCK, **06** ALEXEY SEAFARER/SHUTTERSTOCK, **07** GUGHI/SHUTTERSTOCK, **08** FOTOREQUEST/SHUTTERSTOCK, **09** ROBERT MCGILLIVRAY/SHUTTERSTOCK, **10 & 13** ANDREW M. ALLPORT/SHUTTERSTOCK, **11 & 12** AGAMI PHOTO AGENCY/SHUTTERSTOCK. BACKGROUNDS: SEMPER-SCIFI/SHUTTERSTOCK, PIXUBERANT/SHUTTERSTOCK

Penguins, Seals & Whales

EMBARK ON A WILDLIFE-VIEWING ADVENTURE

The remote Antarctic continent and its surrounding Southern Ocean are home to penguins and seabirds (p118 & p170), seals and whales (p80), which have evolved over eons to thrive in this exceptional environment. Any Antarctica trip is equally a wildlife-viewing adventure at close range. There's nothing like seeing your first whale breach, or a penguin totter along the sea ice.

Left Macaroni penguins **Centre** Royal penguin **Right** Rockhopper penguins

MICHAEL NOLAN/ROBERTHARDING/GETTY IMAGES

Penguin Primer

For many, the word 'Antarctica' immediately conjures up the jolly penguin. Nine species roam the region – some live only on the southern islands and one, the lordly emperor penguin, sticks almost exclusively to the continent. Penguin sexes are similarly marked but sometimes females are smaller. Chicks often huddle in groups called crèches, especially while parents are away hunting.

The Nine Penguins

Adélie Penguins *Pygoscelis adeliae,* the archetypical penguin, is purely black and white, with a distinctive white eye ring. They prefer krill, dive to 150m, create stone-lined nests and take turns protecting two eggs.

Chinstrap Penguins *Pygoscelis antarctica* are black and white with a unique black line below the chin – hence the name. The second-most numerous penguin, after the macaroni, though warming conditions are causing declines, chinstraps feed on krill and fish around the Peninsula and on islands south of the Antarctic Convergence. They lay two eggs in November and chicks fledge by early March.

Gentoo Penguins You can tell the black-and-white *Pygoscelis papua* from the slightly smaller Adélie and chinstrap by its orange bill and white patch above and behind its eye. They are circumpolar, inhabiting subantarctic islands and the Peninsula. Large populations occur at South Georgia (100,000 pairs), Falkland Islands (70,000 pairs) and Îles Kerguelen (30,000 pairs). Gentoos dive over 100m for krill, fish and squid.

Emperor Penguins *Aptenodytes forsteri* is the world's largest penguin, at over 1m (although ancient fossils have

ANDREANITA/SHUTTERSTOCK

REISEGRAF/GETTY IMAGES

been found of penguins measuring 2m) and 40kg. Read more on p128.

King Penguins *Aptenodytes patagonicus* is the second-largest penguin (9kg to 15kg, and 80cm tall). They breed on subantarctic islands, eat primarily lanternfish and squid, and dive to 300m for 15 minutes. For about 55 days in summer, the parents take turns incubating a single egg on their feet in huge colonies. During the long breeding season (14–16 months) chicks are reared through winter.

Macaroni Penguins Orange tassels meeting between the eyes differentiate *Eudyptes chrysolophus* from the smaller (and lighter-billed) rockhopper. This krill-eater is the most abundant of the subantarctic and Antarctic penguins in sometimes gigantic colonies on islands near the Antarctic Convergence and off the Peninsula. They travel up to 10,000km during winter.

Rockhopper Penguins 'Rockies,' the smallest of the crested penguins (2.3kg to 2.7kg), have lemon-yellow tassels that don't meet between the eyes. Subantarctic and temperate-island breeders, they have their largest population on the Falkland Islands. They can breed among boulders where their strong hopping and swimming allow them to transfer easily.

Royal Penguins *Eudyptes schlegeli* are found only at Macquarie Island (p176).

Magellanic Penguins *Spheniscus magellanicus* are a burrowing, brush-tailed species primarily native to the coastal regions of Patagonia (Chile and Argentina). They breed heavily on the sub-Antarctic Falkland Islands.

Help Study Antarctic Wildlife

Antarctic ecosystems are, relatively speaking, simpler than those in other parts of the world. Thus it's easier to observe changes. Though Antarctic life evolved separately, starting with the opening of the Drake Passage millions of years ago, global issues such as pollution, increased UV radiation and climate change are impacting species and ecosystems, giving scientists dynamic areas of study. Disciplines include biochemistry, biology, physiology, genomics and evolution. You can join in by helping identify birds (p168) and marine mammals – upload your photos through the Happywhale (happywhale.com) site, and you'll see their relationships and where they migrate. Maybe you'll meet them again back home!

Seal Spotting

Whether lolling in the sun or diving from the sea ice deep into Antarctica's icy waters, seals provide some of the continent's best wildlife viewing. Vast breeding colonies of elephant and fur seals pack the shores of subantarctic islands like South Georgia, and several of the seven Antarctic species dwell, hidden, in the pack ice. Some are true (earless) seals and others have small flaps over their ears (eg fur seals) and are related to sea lions, which are present in the Falkland Islands. Some breed in colonies, others are restricted to pack ice, and the elusive Ross Seal is hard to spot anywhere.

Seal populations are robust, despite 19th-century hunting. They're protected by the Convention for the Conservation of Antarctic Seals.

The quintessential Antarctic seals, Weddell seals, reach 3.3m and 500kg and live up to 20 years.

The Seven Seals

Antarctic and subantarctic fur seals You'll spot fur seals on most of the circumpolar islands. The Antarctic fur seal (*Arctocephalus gazella;* pictured bottom right) occurs further south than its slightly smaller relative, the subantarctic fur seal *(Arctocephalus tropicalis),* with which it sometimes hybridizes. Males, at more than 200kg and 2m, far outweigh females (55kg and 1.3m). They breed in harems, and males are aggressive to rivals and humans alike. Pupping takes place in December. They eat squid, fish and crustaceans like krill.

Southern elephant seals *Mirounga leonina* is the world's largest seal. Males grow to 3000kg and 5m, females 900kg and 3m. They're on most of the southern islands and the Peninsula. Males fight to determine the 'beachmaster,' with mating rights to a harem of females. Their large proboscis helps create fearsome roars. Adults use their thick blubber layer (for which they were once hunted) to survive while breeding, during which they don't feed (p85).

Weddell seals The quintessential Antarctic seals, *Leptonychotes weddellii* (pictured bottom left) reach 3.3m and 500kg and live up to 20 years. They're circumpolar and live further south than any other mammal (except people), on fast ice (sea ice attached to shore) year-round, and occasionally in pack ice. In October, pups are born in colonies near cracks in the ice that give their mothers access to the sea. Males defend their holes. They also blow air bubbles into the cracks to flush out prey (fish, squid and crustaceans).

Crabeater seals The name 'crabeater' *(Lobodon carcinophaga)* comes from the German word *krebs*, referring to crustaceans, like krill, their almost-exclusive diet (not crab). Their specially adapted teeth with extra projections

BENEDEK/GETTY IMAGES

ROBERT HARDING VIDEO/SHUTTERSTOCK

ADRIAN BOYLE/SHUTTERSTOCK

GERALD CORSI/GETTY IMAGES

form a sieve to strain out krill. These slim seals reach about 2.5m and 400kg, breed in spring on the pack ice and are the world's most abundant seal.

Leopard seals Adult male leopard seals *(Hydrurga leptonyx)* reach 2.8m and 320kg. Females are even larger, at 3.6m and 500kg. Their large heads have huge gapes, making them fearsome predators of penguins, other seals (especially pups), fish, squid and krill. They're in the pack ice in summer and hauled-out on southerly subantarctic islands in winter.

Ross seals *Ommatophoca rossii* dwells in the densest pack ice and is least often seen. Named for its discoverer, James Clark Ross, it's usually found hauled-out onto large floes, alone or in pairs.

Whale Watching

The krill-rich waters of the Southern Ocean attract Earth's largest mammals: baleen whales (which strain krill through fibrous baleen plates lining their jaws). Try to spot rare mighty blue whales and similarly endangered sei whales and southern right whales, though you're more likely see vulnerable fin whales and thriving minkes. You'll recognize humpback whales (pictured above right) by their enormous flippers, which can reach one-third of their body length.

The other type of whales here are toothed whales, such as orca (technically a type of dolphin; pictured above left) and sperm whales (think *Moby Dick*), the largest of the toothed whales, with up to 50 teeth (up to 25cm long) in its lower jaw.

These long-lived, magnificent cetaceans migrate to Antarctic waters each year to feed before returning north to breed. The calves migrate south again with their mothers (for several years until they are independent).

Finding Whales

The **Gerlache Strait** is the Peninsula's crown jewel – humpbacks lunge-feed through krill-dense waters while minkes thread between ice floes. Slip into **Charlotte Bay** or **Wilhelmina Bay** on a glassy day for whales all around.

South Georgia rewards the journey with staggering abundance: humpbacks reclaim feeding grounds their ancestors knew before the whaling era. From **Shag Rocks** to **Cooper Island**, look out to sea...maybe you'll find an elusive blue whale!

The remote **South Orkney Islands** offer unfiltered encounters – fin, humpback and southern right whales compete with a growing krill fishery for the best feeding on the planet.

Dr Ted Cheeseman, *whale biologist and co-founder of Happywhale, has spent 23 seasons in Antarctica.*

17 Northern Gateway of ANTARCTICA

ADÉLIE PENGUINS | VOLCANIC FORMATIONS | SCIENCE BASES

The seldom-visited north of the Antarctica Peninsula, called the Trinity Peninsula, is a land of beautiful rock formations and Adélie penguins. It was claimed by Britain, Chile and Argentina as part of their Antarctic territories. The bases include **Esperanza Station** (Argentina), where the first person was born in Antarctica.

MICHAEL NOLAN/GETTY IMAGES

How to

Get here Check with your operator before booking about how often they actually reach this part of the Peninsula.

First trans-Antarctic flight Aviator Lincoln Ellsworth and copilot Herbert Hollick-Kenyon took off from **Dundee Island** on the first trans-Antarctic flight on November 22, 1935. The trip was to last 14 hours; poor weather stretched it to two weeks. Their monoplane ran out of fuel 25km from the Bay of Whales, and they trekked for eight days. A rescue ship found them at Little America II.

GERALD CORSI/GETTY IMAGES

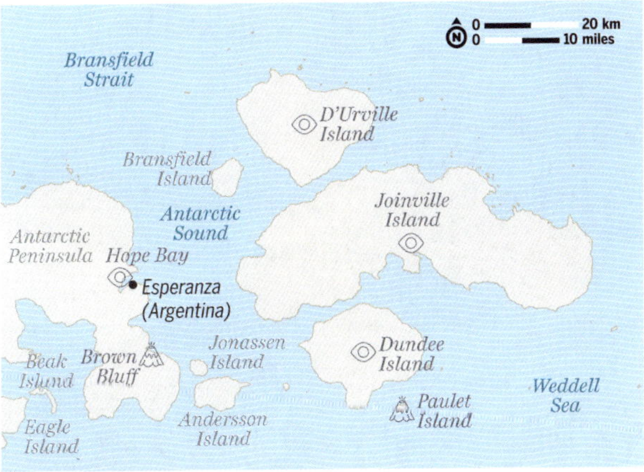

Adélies Among the Volcanoes

Giant Adélie rookery Peep into the northernmost tip of the Peninsula at **Hope Bay** to discover one of Antarctica's largest Adélie rookeries – home to 125,000 pairs, along with a few gentoos. The entrance to the bay via the Antarctic Sound is often filled with tabular icebergs.

Volcanic cliffs Beloved **Brown Bluff** is an ice-capped, flat-topped 745m extinct volcano on the peninsula's northeastern tip. The original diameter of the volcano was about 15km and it's about one million years old. The bluff takes its name from a striking cliff of reddish-brown rock on its north face. Several hundred gentoos and 20,000 Adélies nest here.

Island-dwelling Adélies **Joinville Island**, the largest of the islands at the peninsula's tip, was discovered in 1838 by Dumont d'Urville. At the foot of the reddish 300m-high **Madder Cliffs** (named for the red vegetable dye) 20,000 pairs of Adélies nest. Joinville's northerly neighbor, **D'Urville Island**, was charted by Nordenskjöld in 1902. Circular volcanic **Paulet Island** is just 2km across but its distinctive cone rises 353m high. It was discovered by James Ross' expedition of 1839–43. Enjoy the magnificent rookery of 100,000 pairs of Adélies, and look for visiting blue-eyed shags and southern giant petrels.

Above left Brown Bluff **Bottom left** Antarctic shag, Paulet Island

Nordenskjöld on Paulet Island

On February 12, 1903, Otto Nordenskjöld's ship *Antarctic*, which had been crushed by the Weddell Sea pack ice for weeks, finally sank 40km from Paulet Island. The 20 men sledged for 16 days to reach the island, then built a 10m-by-7m hut on the northeast coast, where all but one survived the winter. Today, the ruins (a pile of stones and some roofing timbers) are populated by Adélies. Marked by a cross, the grave of Ole Christian Wennersgaard, a seaman from the expedition who died of heart disease, lies along the shore 300m east of the hut.

18

Weddell Sea LOST WORLDS

DINOSAURS | EPIC SEA | ICE SHELVES

The Weddell Sea side of the Antarctic Peninsula is surprisingly different from its western side: the mountains rise further back and are fronted by vast, snow-free gravel planes, the ancient province of dinosaurs and giant, prehistoric turtles.

KONRAD WOTHE/GETTY IMAGES

How to

Naming the sea James Weddell discovered the Weddell Sea in February 1823 and named it 'King George IV Sea' for the British sovereign. German Antarctic historian Karl Fricker proposed the name Weddell Sea in 1900.

Plying the sea ice All but the most powerful icebreakers (like Ponant's *Le Commandant Charcot*) are usually prevented from traveling in the Weddell Sea. Others have tried – like Ernest Shackleton (p74) – and paid the price.

Nordenskjöld: A Tale of Luck & Survival

Swedish geologist Otto Nordenskjöld (1869–1928) led expeditions to the Yukon and Tierra del Fuego before helming the 1900 Swedish South Polar Expedition, the first to winter in the Antarctic Peninsula region. Experienced Antarctic explorer Norwegian Carl Larsen captained the *Antarctic*, and by late January 1902, they were exploring the western side of the Peninsula before sailing north around tip, attempting to penetrate the Weddell Sea. Its infamous ice stopped them. Instead Nordenskjöld and five men set up a winter base on **Snow Hill Island** – the hut is still there! Meanwhile, the *Antarctic* sailed to winter in the Falklands before returning, only to be trapped in the ice (p164). Although Nordenskjöld's expedition is remembered for its survival against nearly overwhelming odds, it also performed the most

Above left Adélie penguins, Devil Island (p129) **Below left** Ancient seashells and fossils, Seymour Island (p128)

important Antarctic research up to that time – studying botany, geology, glaciology and hydrography. Read more in *Antarctica: Or Two Years Amongst the Ice of the South Pole* (1905) by Nordenskjöld and Johan Gunnar Andersson.

Giant Penguins & Car-Sized Turtles

Remarkably, 20km-long **Seymour Island** remains ice-free because it lies in the lee of high mountains on neighboring James Ross and Snow Hill Islands. It's the only place in Antarctica with 40- to 120-million-year-old rocks. These reveal one of the most important records of the worldwide 'extinction event' 65 million years ago, which wiped out 70% of the world's species, including the dinosaurs.

While Nordenskjöld wintered at Snow Hill Island he made striking fossil discoveries: the bones of a giant penguin, a find which was confirmed in 1975 by Dr William Zinsmeister. These penguins stood almost 2m tall and weighed up to 135kg. Among the 800

Weddell Sea's Ice Shelves

Filchner-Ronne Ice Shelf
Discovered in 1912, Filchner ice shelf contains Argentina's **Belgrano II Station**, on a 50m nunatak (hill protruding from the ice) 120km from the coast. **Berkner Island** separates Filchner from Ronne Ice Shelf, which is often the start of trans-Antarctic ski trips (p191). The calving of an enormous iceberg in 1998 took Germany's Filchner Station.

Brunt Ice Shelf
Named after astronomer Edmond Halley, **Halley VI** (bas.ac.uk), on the 200m-thick Brunt Ice Shelf, is the most southerly British station. The ice moves about 2m a day, so stations required renewal every decade as they approached the ice edge. Halley VI is designed on skis that allow it to be towed inland.

Giant Sea-Going Reptiles

In addition to the many finds of extinct terrestrial animals, large, extinct marine plesiosaurs have been found on islands near the Peninsula. These long-necked animals with paddle-shaped fins (think Loch Ness Monster) are not dinosaurs but lived at the same time. One of the more spectacular was discovered on Vega Island in 2005.

FROM LEFT: GALLO IMAGES/ORBITAL HORIZON/COPERNICUS SENTINEL DATA 2021 VIA GETTY IMAGES, CHERYLRAMALHO/SHUTTERSTOCK

fossils Zinsmeister found are starfish, crabs, crinoids, corals and nearly 200 new mollusks, among them a 4m-long ammonite. Another interesting discovery: a sea turtle that lived 40 to 45 million years ago and was the size and shape of a Volkswagen Beetle.

James Ross & Vega Islands Dinosaurs

In 1986, the first Antarctic dinosaur discovery was made on **James Ross Island**: a 4m-long *Antarctopelta oliveroi* (an armored dinosaur akin to a stegosaurus). In 1998 a tooth from a hadrosaur (duck-billed dinosaur) was found, and in 2003 a specimen of a 1.8m-long dromeosaurid theropod (a feathered dinosaur) was found on nearby **Vega Island**. Nordenskjöld named the island for the ship *Vega*, used by his uncle Baron AE Nordenskjöld, who made the first crossing of the Northeast Passage in the Arctic in 1878–79. Many other dinosaurs have been unearthed around the Transantarctic Mountains (p126) and mainland.

In summer, snowmelt waterfalls stream down the steep cliff face of Vega's north coast to the scree slopes below – a breathtaking sight, and narrow **Devil Island**, just off its north coast, is home to 12,000 Adélie penguins.

WOLFGANG KAEHLER/LIGHTROCKET VIA GETTY IMAGES

Left Brunt Ice Shelf **Top right** Snow Hill Island (p127) **Bottom right** Snowmelt waterfalls, Vega Island

19 CLIMBING & Epic Adventures

HIGHEST MOUNTAIN | EMPEROR PENGUINS | LUXE EXPEDITIONS

Among Antarctica's high-end adventure expeditions, a climb of Vinson Massif, the continent's highest point, is a perennial bucket-list feat, as are climbs of other remote ranges around the continent. One well-established adventure outfitter flies in to their base camp at Union Glacier and runs high-ticket tours including trips to emperor penguin colonies, South Pole visits and skydiving.

IMAGES & STORIES/ALAMY

How to

Flights to the interior Several companies offer flights to the mainland, followed by guided adventures. These can include a flight or ski to the Pole, or other extravaganzas. Antarctic Logistics & Expeditions (ALE) flies from Punta Arenas, Chile.

Pay the price ALE trips start at an eye-watering US$57,900 for a 12-day Mt Vinson climb or US$64,595 to visit the emperor penguins. Like other high-end adventure providers, they also tailor bespoke trips, with a price tag to match.

SHAIKHSKI/SHUTTERSTOCK

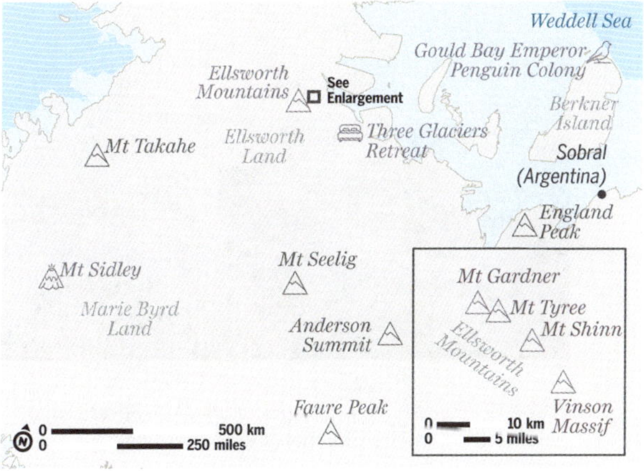

Above left Camping, Vinson Massif
Below left Emperor penguins, Gould Bay

Adventures on the Mainland

Climbing Mt Vinson Antarctica's highest peak is 4897m **Vinson Massif**. The mountain is in the Sentinel Range in the **Ellsworth Mountains**, near the base of the Antarctic Peninsula. It was discovered in 1958 by US Navy aircraft and is named for Congressman Carl Vinson of Georgia, who influenced the US government to support Antarctic exploration from 1935 to 1961. Thanks to the mountaineering pilgrimage of the 'Seven Summits' (scaling the highest peak on each continent), Vinson is also Antarctica's most-climbed mountain.

Since 1985, ALE (antarctic-logistics.com) has guided hundreds of climbers to Vinson's summit. It takes from two to 14 days, depending on weather, and the climber's experience and fitness. Be prepared for all-weather tent camping. Their well-established Union Glacier Camp is the gateway to the Vinson Massif base camp.

Ski safari ALE's Union Glacier Camp and its **Three Glaciers Retreat** are also bases for Union Glacier (p195) climbs, backcountry skiing, cross-country skiing and skydiving.

Make it to the Pole or the emperor penguins ALE has packages that include overnighting at their **camp** at the **Gould Bay Emperor Penguin Colony** on the Weddell Sea, and excursions to the Geographic South Pole (p190), or a climb of Vinson paired with a trip to the South Pole station, with skied portions.

Epic Climbs

On December 18, 1966, four members of a private US expedition led by Nicholas B Clinch made the first ascent of Vinson Massif. Over the next few days, they also reached the summits of Antarctica's second-, third- and fourth-highest peaks: **Mt Tyree** (4852m), **Mt Gardner** (4686m) and **Mt Shinn** (4661m), respectively. Vinson's neighbor, Mt Tyree, is only 45m lower, and it's considered the continent's most challenging peak, but dozens of other Antarctic mountains remain virgin.

ALE runs 12-day trips to climb **Mt Sidley** (4285m), further inland, towards the Ross Sea. It's Antarctica's highest volcano.

■ **By Brekke Fletcher**
Brekke is Senior Director of Content at Lonely Planet. Brekke traveled to Antarctica with support from Silversea cruise lines. Lonely Planet retained full editorial control.
@brekkefletch

Sights, Sounds & Wildlife

THE FIRST THING I LEARNED ABOUT ANTARCTICA IS THAT IMAGINATION IS USELESS THERE.

For months before my trip, I tried to assess what it would feel like to see the southernmost continent. I scrolled through photos of icebergs and penguins, and watched videos of whales surfacing through dark water. None of it came close to the real thing.

Left Lemaire Channel (p107) **Centre** Emperor penguin **Right** Polar plunge

BREKKE FLETCHER/LONELY PLANET

The lesson began the moment our ship, the *Silver Cloud*, entered the Lemaire Channel (p107) after two days crossing the Drake Passage (p90). The crossing had been choppy but manageable – nothing like the horror stories.

On the third morning, Antarctica appeared.

Icebergs drifted past the ship like enormous abstract sculptures. Some were smooth and blue, others jagged and blindingly white. Snow-covered rock rose sharply from the sea. The landscape felt less like a place than a slowly moving gallery of ice.

Passengers wandered the decks in something close to disbelief. For every person trying to capture the moment, affixing lenses and posing for selfies, there were those who simply stared, held hands, hugged. Every exchanged glance seemed to say the same thing: Are we really here?

Our first landing came at Hovgaard Island. After a careful, slippery Zodiac landing in cold gray weather, we stepped onto Antarctic ground and were immediately surrounded by gentoo penguins. They waddled and belly-slid across the snow, comically losing their footing even though this frozen world is their natural habitat. Their squawking echoed across the rocks, accompanied by the unmistakable smell of a large penguin colony.

A few days later, Wilhelmina Bay (p106) offered an entirely different Antarctica. The sky was brilliantly blue and clear, the air crisp, the water calm enough to mirror the icebergs floating around us. Beneath the surface, the ice glowed another shade of luminous blue.

Our Zodiac driver, John, suddenly changed course toward a small iceberg and radioed the other boats. As we

JEREMY FRATKIN

WOLFGANG KAEHLER/ LIGHTROCKET VIA GETTY IMAGES

approached, the reason became clear: an emperor penguin stood alone on the ice.

'We never see emperors here,' John said, grinning.

Three Zodiacs gathered quietly around the berg, engines idling. We patiently and nearly silently took turns photographing our new emperor friend. No one was pushing or hogging the best vantage point. Everyone was generous.

Soon the humpbacks surfaced again, their presence announced by the sudden rush of air from their blowholes. That sound – powerful and alive – became the most beautiful noise I've ever heard.

Moments later, John spotted two humpback whales nearby. The boats repositioned and the mood shifted to quiet anticipation. John coached us on when the whale's tail might rise so we could be ready to take the photos and videos we were all hoping to capture.

Back aboard the ship, the captain slowed the *Silver Cloud* almost to a stop after relocating both the penguin and the whales, giving everyone on board another chance to marvel and swoon.

Standing on our balcony, we waited. Soon the humpbacks surfaced again, their presence announced by the sudden rush of air from their blowholes.

That sound – powerful and alive – became the most beautiful noise I've ever heard.

Even now, remembering it gives me chills.

Taking the Polar Plunge

One of the things I most looked forward to on this expedition was the polar plunge. On the starboard side of the ship, I stripped down to a bathing suit and bare feet while the crew fastened a harness around my waist. From the edge of a Zodiac, I jumped. The shock of the water – just a few degrees above freezing – hit instantly. I surfaced flailing, shouting expletives and made a very undignified swim to the ladder. Within seconds I was climbing out, adrenaline surging. Strangely, I wasn't that cold once I got out. I didn't even need a robe. The plunge was bracing, hilarious, unforgettable.

ROSS SEA

HISTORY | WILDLIFE | REMOTE

RESEARCHED BY LIZ CARLSON

At Cape Adare, see **Borchgrevink's huts** (p143) and the **Adélie penguin colony** (p150)

At the **Drygalski Ice Tongue**, view massive glacial calvings (p159)

Visit Shackleton's **Nimrod hut** on Ross Island (p144)

ROSS SEA
Trip Builder

The Ross Sea is defined by immense scale and remoteness, where wildlife thrives beside vast ice shelves and open horizons as it did during the Heroic Age. It holds Antarctica's richest historic heritage, penguin colonies and pristine marine ecosystems, overlooked by towering Mt Erebus.

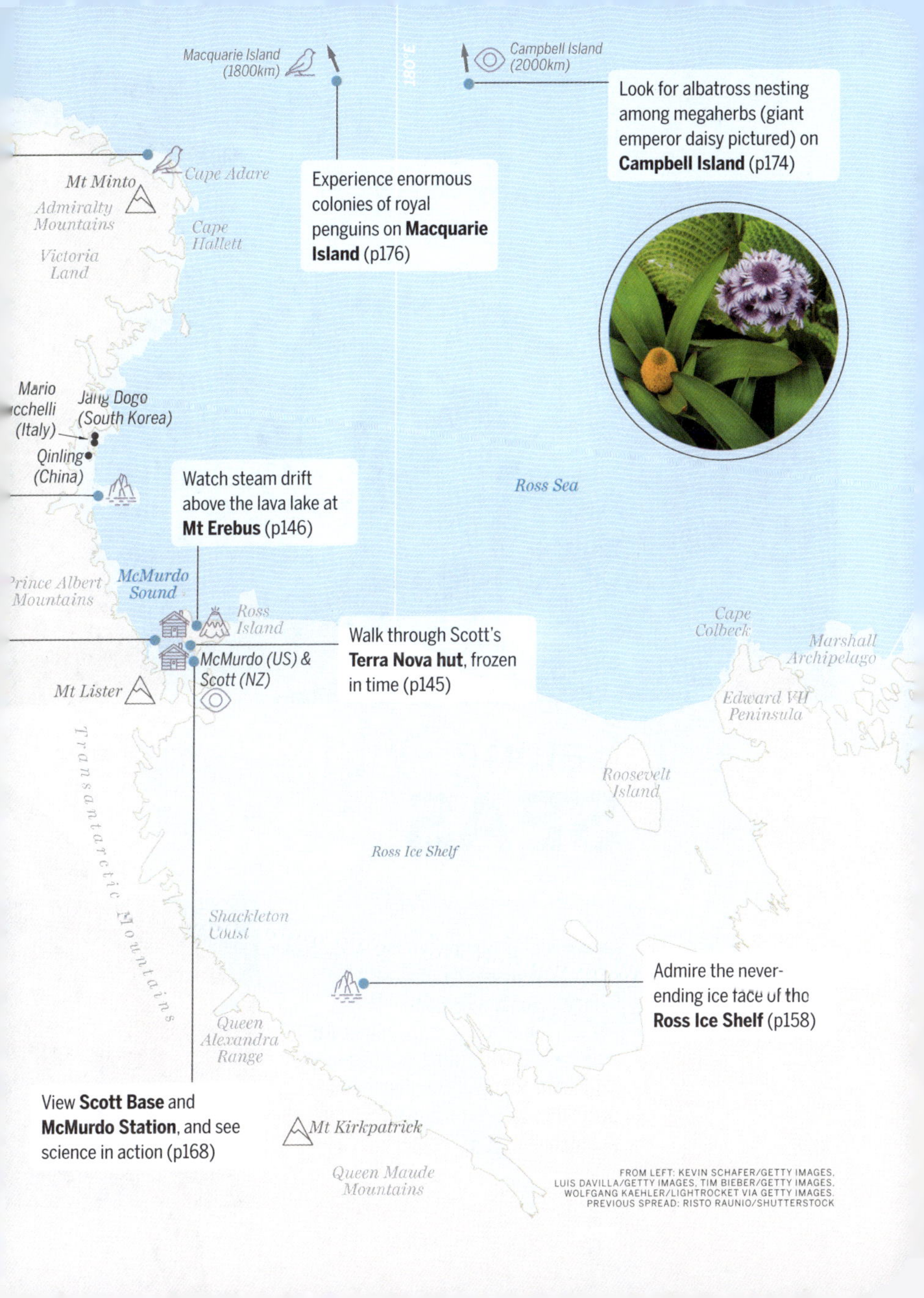

FROM LEFT: KEVIN SCHAFER/GETTY IMAGES, LUIS DAVILLA/GETTY IMAGES, TIM BIEBER/GETTY IMAGES, WOLFGANG KAEHLER/LIGHTROCKET VIA GETTY IMAGES. PREVIOUS SPREAD: RISTO RAUNIO/SHUTTERSTOCK

20 Sailing Wild SEAS

WHALES | BIRDS | WAVES

The journey to the Ross Sea is an adventure in and of itself. There's no denying that these seas are not known for their fine weather. But among the big swells and wild waves, there are whales, dolphins and an abundance of seabirds.

IMAGE PROFESSIONALS GMBH/ALAMY

Buckle Up

There is an old sailing proverb that goes along the lines of 'below 40° S, there is no law; below 50° S, there is no God.' The Drake Passage tends to get the attention when it comes to sea crossings to Antarctica. The truth is, any open crossing around these latitudes can be wild; they can also be calm.

As a general rule, the open seas have bigger swells (for example, crossing between **Macquarie Island** and the Antarctic continent), and then it's more sheltered closer to shore. The expedition ships that ferry you southwards have never been more comfortable, with built-in stabilizers and other features to make the crossings more pleasant.

How to

When to go Sea ice conditions are most navigable from January to February.

Duration and cost Ross Sea expeditions start around US$30,000 and range from 22–34 days.

Get out on deck Ships don't always announce wildlife spottings so spend time on deck on crossings.

Operators Heritage Expeditions (heritage-expeditions.com) has sailed the Ross Sea annually for decades, while others visit more sporadically: Ponant (ponant.com), Aurora Expeditions (aurora-expeditions.com), Scenic (scenic.com), Swan Hellenic (swanhellenic.com) and Hapag-Lloyd Cruises (hl-cruises.com).

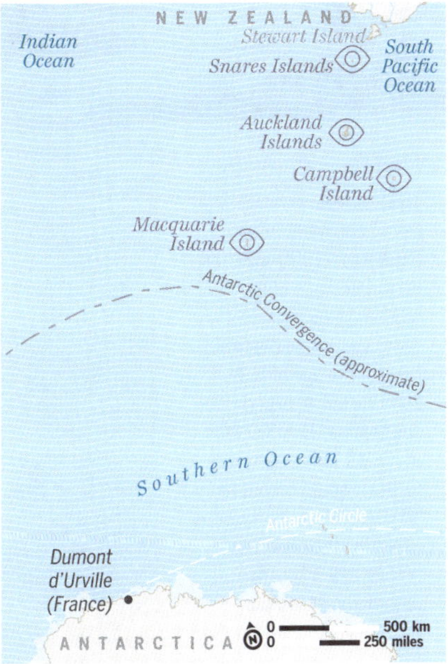

Above left Hapag-Lloyd Cruise's ship crashing through waves
Below left Antipodean albatross (p141)

Follow the Great Explorers

Many of the iconic explorers, such as Robert Falcon Scott, Ernest Shackleton and Roald Amundsen, departed from New Zealand and Australia, their last provisioning stop, en route to the Ross Sea. Desperate to conserve coal, they sailed southwards, with Shackleton even organizing the *Nimrod* to be towed south most of the way. In fact, Douglas Mawson was famously sick for his entire first voyage down south. Shortly after departing New Zealand, Scott's *Terra Nova* was caught in a violent storm that nearly overwhelmed the ship. During the chaos, one of the sled dogs was swept overboard, only to be washed back onto the deck by the next wave.

Whale-Watching Territory

Some of the best wildlife viewing can be from the expedition ship's decks. In the warmer waters of the subantarctic, you might see hourglass dolphins, long-finned pilot whales

James Clark Ross

The Ross Sea gets its name from Scotsman James Clark Ross (1800–62), considered one of the most dashing figures of his time, who joined the Royal Navy at the age of 11. In 1839, he led an expedition south aboard HMS *Erebus* and HMS *Terror*, setting a furthest-south record for 50 years. After two seasons exploring the region and setting a new southern record, the expedition returned to England in 1843. Both ships were later lost in John Franklin's ill-fated Northwest Passage expedition in the Arctic. Ross later briefly returned north to search for Franklin.

The Threatened Antipodean Albatross

The broader threats facing albatross populations are evident in the Antipodean albatross. Over the past few decades, three-quarters have disappeared. The decline continues, largely due to climate change and longline-fishing bycatch; males now outnumber females three to one.

DR JOHN A HORSFALL/GETTY IMAGES

and, if you're lucky, southern right whales. As you sail southwards around the Antarctic Convergence (where warmer waters meet the cold waters of the Antarctic), you could see more baleen whales, like humpbacks or even blue whales. In open seas, you'll usually spot the whale's blow before you see the whale itself. Look for blows in the distance; they have different shapes depending on the whale type.

An Abundance of Seabirds

On open-sea days, as ships travel between destinations, you can enjoy great pelagic birding. Many seabirds are known for following ships and one of the best places to birdwatch is the back deck.

You might see large royal or light-mantled albatross circling the ship on the open seas. Albatross can spend years at sea, traveling tens of thousands of kilometers. Because they glide, they need wind to help them travel. Calm sea days usually mean fewer albatross.

Giant petrels are often about, and many other petrel species and Antarctic prions can be seen alongside the ship. As you approach the continent, you might see more snow petrels and skuas.

FROM LEFT: ARTHUR GREENBERG/ALAMY, RICHARD MCMANUS/GETTY IMAGES

Clockwise from far left Humpback whale; Antarctic prion; Hourglass dolphin

21 STEP INTO Heroic Age Huts

HISTORY | REMOTE | EXPLORERS

The star of Antarctica's heroic age of exploration is the Ross Sea. Here, intrepid explorers like Scott and Shackleton established their bases to conquer the South Pole. Only by entering their historic huts can you truly sense what it must have been like on early expeditions.

CINDY HOPKINS/ALAMY

How to

Getting here Historic huts can only be visited by expedition ship. Zodiac landings and conditions determine which sites are accessible.

When to go Sea ice is lowest in January and February, making the huts more accessible.

What to wear Visitor numbers are limited in the huts, so you may need to wait outside. Be sure to dress warmly.

More info Learn more on the Antarctic Heritage Trust website (nzaht.org).

Exploration at Borchgrevink's Huts

The first buildings erected in Antarctica are located on Cape Adare and were part of Carsten Borchgrevink's *Southern Cross* expedition (1898–1900). The first to overwinter on shore in Antarctica, 10 men lived in **Borchgrevink's Huts** with 90 dogs, conducting scientific research and surveys. A smaller stores hut to the west is now roofless. It contains boxes of ammunition that Borchgrevink brought in case the expedition encountered large predators such as polar bears. (He was the first to winter here and had no idea what lay ahead).

Behind the hut is **Hanson's Grave**, marking the burial of Nicolai Hanson, the first person to die on the continent. Today, the huts are completely surrounded by an Adélie penguin colony.

Above & below left Shackleton's Hut (p144), Cape Royds

Inside Scott's Discovery Hut

Built for Robert Falcon Scott's first expedition to Antarctica (1901–04), the **Discovery Hut** is located near two main research hubs: McMurdo Station and Scott Base. Scott's *Discovery* expedition was large and marked a turning point in British exploration down south. Scott's men never used the hut for accommodation because it was difficult to heat. Instead, it was used for storage, repair work and as an entertainment center (called 'The Royal Terror Theatre'). It was a key base used by later expeditions.

See Shackleton's Hut

The *Nimrod* expedition erected **Shackleton's Hut** on Cape Royds. Fifteen men called this place home for 14 months, and the feeling here is still very atmospheric. Inside, you can find Shackleton's signature (which may or may not be authentic) in his tiny bunk room, along with food tins and even socks

The Worst Journey in the World

In winter 1911, three members of Scott's *Terra Nova* expedition undertook one of the most grueling journeys in polar exploration. Aiming for Cape Crozier, their brutal trek from Cape Evans, through darkness and extreme cold, was later immortalized by Apsley Cherry-Garrard in his classic account *The Worst Journey in the World*. With Edward Wilson and 'Birdie' Bowers, they braved 24-hour darkness and temperatures as low as -59°C, so cold that their chattering teeth broke off. They hoped to collect emperor penguin embryos, believing they might reveal an evolutionary link between reptiles and birds. The three eggs they gathered are in London's Natural History Museum.

A Whisky Surprise

In January 2010, in a sensational find, conservators unearthed three crates of Mackinlay's whisky and two crates of brandy from under Shackleton's Hut. After they had been thawed in Christchurch in 2011, the master blender at Whyte & Mackay (owners of the Mackinlay's brand) in Scotland analyzed and replicated the expedition's whisky precisely.

FROM LEFT: CINDY HOPKINS/ALAMY, PEACE PORTAL PHOTO/ALAMY

with holes in them. It's situated next to Pony Lake, named for the Manchurian ponies that accompanied the expedition, along with dogs for hauling gear. It didn't work out well for the ponies.

Outside the hut lie the remnants of the pony stables and the garage built for the Arrol-Johnson motorcar (Antarctica's first car). Since then, the hut has undergone an extensive conservation project by the Antarctic Heritage Trust.

Tour Scott's Final Expedition Hut

The largest of the huts on Ross Island in 1911, **Scott's Hut** was constructed during his *Terra Nova* expedition. Built to support his ill-fated journey to the South Pole, this historic hut on Cape Evans has been carefully restored from the box of penguin eggs to the telephone that connected the men to the *Discovery* Hut. Perched next to a volcanic black-sand beach with Mt Erebus looming in the distance, it evokes the feeling that the explorers might return at any minute. Occupied later by the Ross Sea party of Shackleton's *Endurance* expedition, there is a memorial cross nearby to commemorate the three men who perished on the supply depot journey.

CINDY HOPKINS/ALAMY

Left Scott's Hut from the *Terra Nova* expedition
Above right Scott's Discovery Hut
Below right Molting Adélie penguins at Borchgrevink's Huts (p143)

22 Meet Mt EREBUS

VOLCANO | VIEWS | SCENERY

Impressive Mt Erebus, the world's most southerly active volcano, is 3794m high. Its lazily drifting plume of steam is a familiar sight throughout the Ross Sea region, as it overlooks so many of the area's iconic spots. Erebus is notable for its persistent lava lake, one of only a handful on Earth, and has remained continuously active since it was first observed.

DOUG ALLAN/GETTY IMAGES

How to

Getting there Expedition trips to the Ross Sea (January to February) will see Mt Erebus dominating the horizon. It can often be seen on scenic flights from Australia.

Look for the plume During the midnight sun, soft light hitting the steam from the crater makes an excellent photo.

Read more Colin Monteath's book *Erebus the Ice Dragon: Portrait of an Antarctic Volcano* combines great imagery and stories around the science, history and exploration of Mt Erebus.

ALASDAIR TURNER, GOLF 4-3-9 ANTARCTICA EXPEDITION 2012/WIKIMEDIA/CC BY 4.0

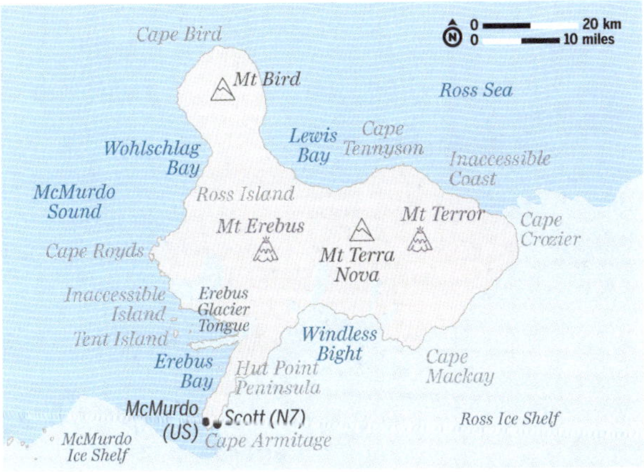

Discoveries The first record was in 1841 by Sir James Clark Ross, who named it after his ship, HMS *Erebus*; the extinct volcano alongside it was named **Mt Terror** after Ross' second ship, HMS *Terror*. He noted that it was erupting at the time. **Mt Erebus** was first climbed in 1908 by a party from Shackleton's *Nimrod* expedition.

Steam and lava pools Situated on Ross Island, Mt Erebus is a constant presence on the horizon on a voyage to the Ross Sea, with steam billowing up from its peak in spite of the stratovolcano being covered in snow and ice. One of the largest volcanoes in the world, it is unique in that it's one of the few with an ever-present active lava lake with a temperature of 1000°C (1832°F). A geological curiosity, Erebus emits about 80g of metallic gold crystals each day. A heat-resistant enzyme from microbes on Mt Erebus helps scientists copy DNA quickly, speeding up forensic testing.

Somber history Mt Erebus is infamous as the site of Antarctica's worst air tragedy. All 257 people aboard Air New Zealand flight 901 were killed when their DC-10 slammed into the base of the volcano above Lewis Bay on November 28, 1979. The Antarctic Treaty countries have declared the crash site a tomb. One edge of the site is marked by a stainless-steel cross.

Above left Mt Erebus **Below left** Fumarolic ice tower, Mt Erebus

Ice & Steam

Mt Erebus' summit features beautiful fumarolic ice towers. From sea level, these can be observed with binoculars on the volcano's upper summit plateau. The ice towers represent places where heated, water-rich gases vent to the surface along fractures. When the gas reaches the cold air, the water freezes and forms bizarre shapes. Towers, tunnels and caves are common, melted into the underlying snow and ice. These ice caves are warm and steamy and, in some cases, feel like a sauna. During the summer, when the sun dips toward the horizon around midnight, the ice towers look spectacular as steam slowly ascends through the hollow towers and vents out the top.

23

Wildlife on the ICE EDGE

BIODIVERSITY | NATURE | PENGUINS

The Ross Sea feels like Antarctica turned up a notch. Ice-heavy, remote and far from the busier Peninsula routes, it's home to some of the most cold-adapted wildlife along with some of the largest penguin colonies on the planet.

RISTO RAUNIO/SHUTTERSTOCK

How to

Getting there Sea ice generally breaks up from January to February. You'll see wildlife from the expedition ship, Zodiac; on shore during landings; or out on the ice.

Biosecurity Where there are penguin colonies, there is a risk of accidentally transmitting introduced species or diseases from your gear, especially boots. All ships follow rigorous biosecurity protocols (p227).

Top tip Bring good binoculars; they're great for whale watching and looking for seabirds.

JASON EDWARDS/GETTY IMAGES

Walk with Emperor Penguins

Emperor penguins are the largest penguin species in the world, and are considered one of only two 'true' Antarctic penguins (along with Adélie). Some of your best chances of seeing them are in the Ross Sea, where they have breeding colonies nearby. While visiting the colonies themselves isn't usually possible, you're most likely to see them either on their own or in small groups. If conditions allow, you can sometimes land on fast ice – the sea ice fixed to the coast that does not move – where you can walk with the emperors.

They are the only Antarctic bird that breeds in winter and that can only be found south of the Antarctic Convergence. A single egg is incubated on the males' feet, who group-huddle in the extreme winter cold to reduce heat loss. Meanwhile, females travel across the ice

LUIS DAVILLA/GETTY IMAGES

The Mysterious Ross Seal

The Ross seal is the rarest of the Antarctic seals. Seen sporadically around the Ross Sea, they live in the densest pack ice, making them the least-studied seal species. Small with big eyes, they have silvery coats marked with black streaks. Known for distinctive vocalizations, they're at the top of many wildlife bucket lists.

Above left Adélie penguin colony, off Cape Adare (p150) **Left** Crabeater seal (p151) **Above** Minke whale (p151), McMurdo Sound

to feed. There are roughly 250,000 breeding pairs and their numbers are declining.

The Biggest Adélie Penguin Colony

Sprawled across the shore of Cape Adare is the **Adélie penguin colony** long considered to be Antarctica's largest, home to over one million penguins. Megacolonies have since been discovered via satellite in other locations. Cape Hallett is also home to a large colony of Adélies.

The archetypical Antarctic penguin was named by French explorer Dumont d'Urville after his wife. Purely black and white, Adélies have a distinctive white eye ring and are known for their curiosity. Just remember: big colonies of birds mean a lot of guano, a smell you'll never forget.

Orca Galore

There are four different types of orca found in Antarctica. The Ross Sea is home to type C,

Ross Sea Region Marine Protected Area

The Ross Sea is considered to be one of the best-preserved ecosystems on Earth, with minimal human impact and disturbance. It's home to a third of the world's Adélie penguins and a quarter of the world's emperor penguins. There are six species of krill, over 200 species of sponges, 12 species of whales and even a starfish with 50 arms. Recognizing its unique biodiversity, New Zealand and the United States led the efforts to establish the Ross Sea region Marine Protected Area (MPA) in 2017. The world's largest MPA, it covers 1.55 million sq km.

JASON EDWARDS/GETTY IMAGES

Clockwise from far left Emperor penguins (p149) near a crack in the sea ice; Orcas, McMurdo Sound; Molting juvenile emperor penguin (p149)

FROM LEFT: BRIAN L STETSON/SHUTTERSTOCK, COLIN HARNISH/SHUTTERSTOCK

the smallest of the orca, reaching up to 6m long. It's common to see them around McMurdo Sound, hunting Antarctic toothfish along the ice edge. They can be inquisitive, spy hopping by lifting their heads from the water to observe the area, and checking out the boats. Other cetaceans frequent the waters here as well, including minkes, humpbacks, fin and even blue whales. Orcas are well-adapted to life around sea ice and are often seen moving along the pack ice. They are among the most frequently encountered whales in the Ross Sea region.

Check Out All the Seals

Many Antarctic headliners can be spotted in the Ross Sea. Seals are the most common marine mammal found here, and the Ross Sea is home to the largest concentration of Weddell seals in the world; they're a common sight on the pack ice. The most common seal in the world, the crabeater, can also be frequently seen on the ice. Solitary apex predators, leopard seals are a highlight for many people, especially when hunting. Their large reptilian-like heads make them easy to distinguish from other seals. Even the occasional elephant seal can be spotted from time to time.

Polar Rations

WHAT EXPLORERS ATE DURING THE HEROIC AGE

Explorers' diets during the Heroic Age left much to be desired. Expeditions began with good intentions, with provisions for multiple years down south. They took advantage of what Mother Nature provided: penguins and seals – when eaten fresh, raw or lightly cooked – provided the vitamin C needed to survive.

POPPERFOTO VIA GETTY IMAGES/GETTY IMAGES

Inside the huts, meals were similar to back home, but they lacked fresh ingredients – with most fruit, vegetables and meat coming from cans. A perfectly preserved 100-year-old fruitcake was even found at one of the huts on Cape Adare. Before winter set in, they cached a large supply of meat once the wildlife disappeared. Controversial polar explorer Frederick Cook – later accused of fraud for faking the first ascent of Mount McKinley (Denali) and for fabricating his claim to have reached the North Pole – described the taste of penguin: 'If it is possible to imagine a piece of beef and odiferous codfish and a canvasback duck roast in a pot with blood and cod liver oil for sauce, the illustration would be complete.'

After enduring a long winter in their prefabricated huts, explorers like Shackleton, Amundsen and Scott would set off surveying, conducting scientific research and, of course, aiming to tackle the South Pole. Teams would lay food and fuel depots along the way for them to use on the return to base. But often things didn't go according to plan: stores would be lost. The men would get stuck for longer than planned. They didn't bring enough provisions. And inevitably, they didn't calculate the proper calorie intake for such a hostile environment. As Shackleton famously wrote on his *Nimrod* expedition, 'Our food lies ahead, and death stalks us from behind.' With scurvy and starvation always lingering nearby, they would eat just about anything.

Only Amundsen was exempt, thanks to his rigorous planning and polar knowledge gained from his time on the *Belgica* and in the Arctic. His party actually gained weight on the return journey from the South Pole.

Left Scott's team laying a depot for their return to base **Centre** A tin of pemmican, sledging biscuits and hoosh **Right** Cook Thomas Clissold, *Terra Nova* hut

Pemmican

Along with butter, cocoa and tea, pemmican was the staple in an explorer's diet a century ago. The most common sledging ration, pemmican originated among the Cree and other Indigenous peoples of North America. A dense food made from dried meat, fat and sometimes berries, it provided high energy in small portions and remained edible for years. They also had special pemmican for their sled dogs, which they sometimes ended up eating themselves... along with the dogs. In the historic huts (p142), you can often see the provisions left behind, with some brands still around today. Bovril and Heinz feature prominently.

> 'Our food lies ahead, and death stalks us from behind.' With scurvy and starvation always lingering nearby, they would eat just about anything.

Sledging Biscuits

The other core component of diets out in the field was sledging biscuits. Long-lasting, dense and high-energy, they took the place of bread while out sledging, similar to the hardtack (dense crackers) eaten by sailors. Some biscuit brands included powdered milk extract known as Plasmon.

Hoosh

If you mix sledging biscuits, pemmican and melted snow together, you have a kind of soup called hoosh, a core part of the sledging diet, especially when they needed something warm to eat.

Christmas Pudding

'I must write a word of our supper last night. We had four courses. The first, pemmican, full whack, with slices of horse meat flavoured with onion and curry powder and thickened with biscuit; then an arrowroot, cocoa and biscuit hoosh sweetened; then a plum-pudding; then cocoa with raisins, and finally a dessert of caramels and ginger. After the feast it was difficult to move. Wilson and I couldn't finish our share of plum-pudding. We have all slept splendidly and feel thoroughly warm – such is the effect of full feeding.'

From Robert Falcon Scott's diary on the Terra Nova expedition, 1911

24 Mighty ICEBERGS

ICE | BLUE | SCENERY

Your first introduction to Antarctica will likely be an iceberg drifting past the ship as you head south. The Antarctic ice sheet is the iceberg factory of the Southern Ocean, calving about 2300 cu km of ice annually with an estimated 300,000 icebergs at any given time.

BIOSPHOTO/ALAMY

How to

Safety Only 8–10% of an iceberg is visible above water. Zodiacs keep their distance from icebergs (especially large ones) as they could extend far out under the water and cause tsunamis when they flip or break apart.

Calvings When glaciers calve or icebergs break apart, you can often hear it before you see it. It can sound like gunshots or thunder.

Cloudy days Icebergs appear even bluer under softer, diffused light.

COPYRIGHT JEFF MILLER/GETTY IMAGES

Tabular vs Non-Tabular

Icebergs are split into two categories: tabular and non-tabular. Tabular icebergs break off from ice shelves and have vertical, steep sides and a flat top. They can be enormous, and historically, some of the largest tabular icebergs have come from the Ross Ice Shelf. Non-tabular icebergs calve off from glaciers and can vary widely in size. Individual icebergs range in dimension from a few meters long (growlers) to 5–10m long (bergy bits) to hundreds of meters long. You will see a lot more tabular icebergs in the Ross Sea than on the Peninsula because of the proximity to ice shelves.

10CBOON/SHUTTERSTOCK

Zodiac Cruise Around Icebergs

A quintessential Antarctic experience is cruising around icebergs. They come in all

Antarctica's Green Icebergs

Green icebergs are a rare sight in Antarctica. Their jade color comes from marine ice, formed when deep seawater rich in organic material freezes onto the underside of ice shelves under deep pressure with no air bubbles. When an iceberg flips that came from these shelves, this clear, green marine layer reveals its vivid underside.

Above left Snow petrel flying by a tabular iceberg **Below left** Non-tabular iceberg **Above** Green iceberg

shapes and sizes, and sometimes you can see spectacular iceberg arches or caves. You'll see them from the expedition ship but also on Zodiac cruises. Occasionally, you see patches of black, sediment or even rocks on icebergs that were picked up when the ice was moving on land. Wildlife often takes advantage of icebergs, with penguins and seals perched on the ice. It's hard to imagine how penguins make it onto the top of a tall iceberg, but they're remarkably agile. They porpoise through the water at speed and can launch themselves upward, using their strong, clawed feet and sharp nails to grip the ice and pull themselves onto the surface. However, they don't always make it the first time...

Why So Blue?

Icebergs can appear blue because of the way light interacts with dense glacial ice. As snow accumulates over thousands of years, it becomes compressed and denser, forcing

Iceberg Names

When icebergs break off from ice shelves as tabular blocks, they can be hundreds of kilometers long. They're tracked and named by the US National Ice Center using a simple system: the letter refers to the Antarctic quadrant where the iceberg first calved (A, B, C or D), the number indicates its sequence, and a lowercase letter is added if it breaks into pieces. Iceberg A-23a, for example, calved in the A sector and is the 23rd iceberg recorded there, with 'a' marking it as a fragment of the original. It was the largest iceberg in the world (twice the size of Greater London) until recently – it broke up near South Georgia.

RICHARD MCMANUS/GETTY IMAGES

Clockwise from far left Iceberg A-23a; Striped iceberg in Terra Nova Bay; Person standing near an iceberg

FROM LEFT: MODIS LAND RAPID RESPONSE TEAM, NASA GSFC/WIKIMEDIA/PUBLIC DOMAIN; BRIAN L STETSON/SHUTTERSTOCK

out most of the trapped air and forming clear ice. Without air bubbles to scatter light, sunlight can penetrate deeper. Ice absorbs longer-wavelength light, such as red and yellow, more easily than it absorbs blue light. The blue light travels further through the ice and reflects back to our eyes, giving icebergs their vivid color. The older and more compact the ice, the more intense the blue appears.

Striped Icebergs

Striped icebergs form when seawater seeps into cracks and crevasses on the underside of floating ice shelves and then freezes. This process creates layers of marine ice that differ from the glacial ice above. Because marine ice forms from seawater under pressure, it often contains traces of organic material. When an iceberg calves, these layers can become visible as distinct bands. The original glacial ice, formed from compressed snowfall, tends to appear lighter and more opaque, while frozen seawater can appear as darker blue or even green stripes. The contrast between bubbly, milky glacial ice and the clearer marine ice creates the dramatic striped effect seen in some Antarctic icebergs.

25 SAIL THE Ross Ice Shelf

ICE | PHOTOGRAPHY | VAST

Covering 520,000 sq km, an area roughly the size of France, the Ross Ice Shelf is one of the most impressive sites in the Ross Sea. The largest ice shelf in Antarctica floats over the ocean and stretches over 600km long. It was named after James Clark Ross, who first spotted it.

How to

Getting there Best viewed on a cruise: you're more elevated and can get closer to the face. Expedition ships with helicopters, like Scenic (scenic.com), might try to land on the top.

Many names Originally called the Barrier, it was named the Victoria Barrier in honor of Queen Victoria. Since then, it has been called the Great Barrier, Great Ice Barrier, Great Southern Barrier, Icy Barrier, Ross Ice Barrier, and, these days, the Ross Ice Shelf.

JOSH LANDIS/NATIONAL SCIENCE FOUNDATION/AFP VIA GETTY IMAGES

Clockwise from bottom left
Drygalski Ice Tongue; Ross Ice Shelf viewed from a cruise boat; Iceberg D 16

Discovery of the Ross Ice Shelf

History Discovered on January 28, 1841 by James Clark Ross while searching for the South Magnetic Pole, the **Ross Ice Shelf** forms a near-vertical face rising up to 50m above sea level. Because it dips so far inland, it's geographically closer to the South Pole, making it the gateway for those chasing the highest latitudes. Shackleton's party was the first to cross it as they tried to reach the South Pole. In 1911, both Amundsen and Scott used the Ross Ice Shelf, on opposite sides, to access the interior, where they both reached the South Pole. Scenic offers sightseeing helicopter flights onto the Ross Ice Shelf (additional cost) if conditions permit.

Where icebergs are born The shelf moves as fast as 1.1km per year, and calves an estimated 150 cu km of icebergs annually, out of its total of 23,000 cu km of ice. A giant iceberg, named B-15, calved in March 2000. Measuring 298km by 37km and covering an area of about 11,000 sq km, it was the largest iceberg ever recorded. Scientists regard the calving of giant icebergs as part of a process whereby the ice sheet maintains a balance between constant outward growth from the continent and periodic loss from iceberg calving. The recent acceleration of the calving, though, is due to the effects of climate change.

Drygalski Ice Tongue

Discovered by Scott in 1902, the Drygalski Ice Tongue was named for German Antarctic explorer Professor Erich von Drygalski, with whom Scott coordinated operations before his first expedition. This 4000-year-old floating ice tongue is the extension of the David Glacier jutting 70km out to sea, and is a great place to see calvings. The largest ice tongue in Antarctica is best viewed on a ship cruise alongside it, which gives you a sense of scale. It's been hit twice by enormous icebergs, knocking significant chunks off of it; the latest piece is the reason Commonwealth Bay has been inaccessible for years.

26 UNDER the Midnight Sun

REMOTE | SEA | ADVENTURE

One of the major lines of latitude, the Antarctic Circle sits at 66°33′ S. It's the southernmost point where the sun stays above the horizon for one day in summer. It's a rite of passage for those traveling to the Ross Sea.

JOHN BROWN/GETTY IMAGES

How to

Dress warm The Ross Sea lies further south than the Peninsula so it's much colder.

Distance Crossing the Drake Passage takes two days; sailing from New Zealand can take eight days with no stops. This is the main reason Ross Sea trips are more costly than Peninsula trips.

On the move The Antarctic Circle moves slightly every year because the Earth's axial tilt slowly changes over time.

Pack Bring a good eyemask to block sunlight.

DAI MAR TAMARACK/SHUTTERSTOCK

Cross the Antarctic Circle

Captain James Cook was the first to cross the Antarctic Circle, the invisible gateway to Antarctica, on January 17, 1773, on board the HMS *Resolution*. The circle marks the latitude where the sun can remain above the horizon for 24 hours during the Antarctic summer. All trips to the Ross Sea will cross the Antarctic Circle on their voyage south, and it's usually celebrated.

GALEN ROWELL/MOUNTAIN LIGHT/ALAMY

Polar Plunge

Another longstanding Antarctic expedition tradition is doing a polar plunge. A trip to the Ross Sea voyages well below the Antarctic Circle, which means this will be a true polar plunge. It can happen whenever there is time in the itinerary under calm conditions, varying ship to ship. Sometimes you jump off a

Terra Australis Incognita

Antarctica was imagined long before it was discovered. Ancient Greek thinkers such as Aristotle believed the lands of the north must be balanced by a southern continent, an idea later known as Terra Australis Incognita, meaning the unknown southern land. Ptolemy even mapped a large southern continent around 150 CE.

Above left Weddell seals
Below left Mt Erebus (p146) **Above** Orcas

Zodiac, other times from the gangway or side gate. Certain ships rope you up, in case you need to be hauled back aboard, and there are always safety teams and medical personnel on hand to help.

Polar plunges are optional but fairly popular, especially on sunny days, usually with an audience cheering everyone on from the upper decks. The expedition photographer is placed nearby to get shots of everyone jumping. There's usually great music playing, dry towels and a shot of something to warm you up. For couples jumping together, it can be a true test of character, whether you graciously let your partner climb out first or make a determined dash for the ladder yourself.

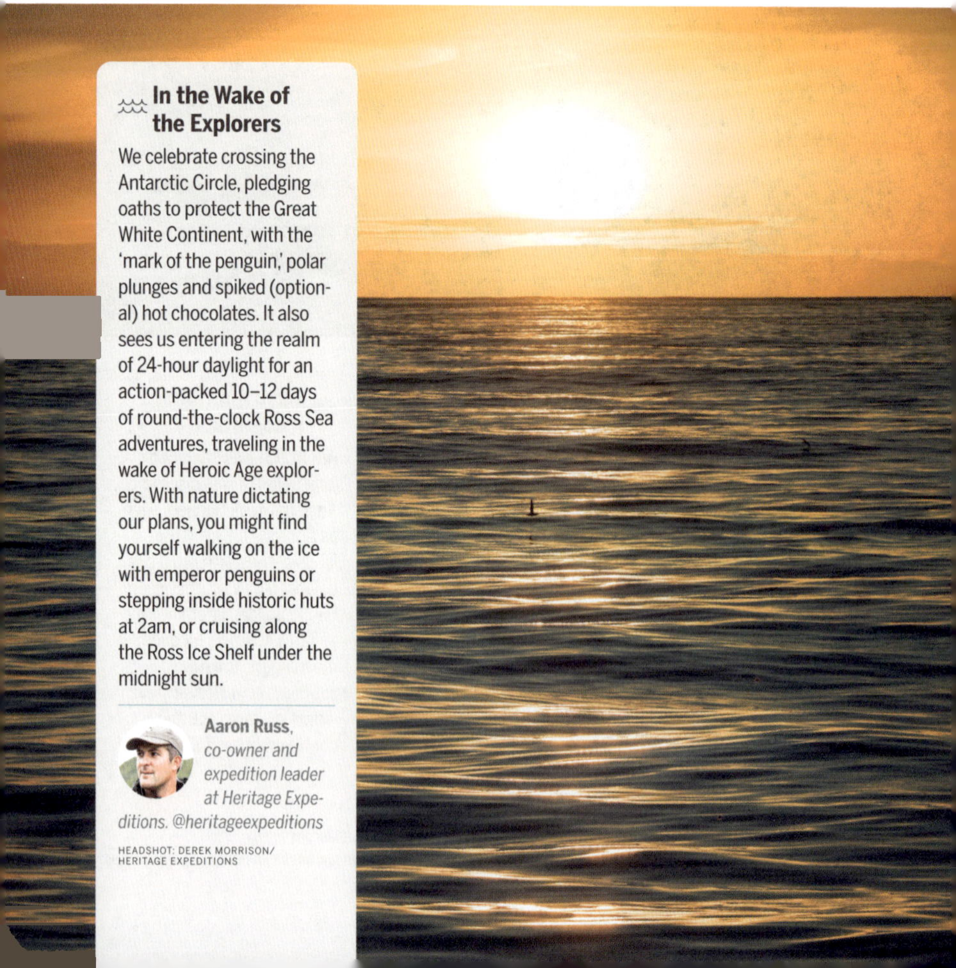

In the Wake of the Explorers

We celebrate crossing the Antarctic Circle, pledging oaths to protect the Great White Continent, with the 'mark of the penguin,' polar plunges and spiked (optional) hot chocolates. It also sees us entering the realm of 24-hour daylight for an action-packed 10–12 days of round-the-clock Ross Sea adventures, traveling in the wake of Heroic Age explorers. With nature dictating our plans, you might find yourself walking on the ice with emperor penguins or stepping inside historic huts at 2am, or cruising along the Ross Ice Shelf under the midnight sun.

Aaron Russ, *co-owner and expedition leader at Heritage Expeditions. @heritageexpeditions*

HEADSHOT: DEREK MORRISON/ HERITAGE EXPEDITIONS

LIZ CARLSON

Clockwise from far left Calm sea under a midnight sun; Polar plunge (p161); On deck the *Kapitan Khlebnikov*

Midnight Sun

The further south you travel, the more midnight sun you'll have. Since Ross Sea trips usually take place in January and February, you will have a lot of midnight sun, when the sun never dips below the horizon. When you are in places like McMurdo Sound in January, the sun circles the horizon, and in February, the sun will begin to dip slightly below the horizon, though it won't get fully dark. The lighting at these times makes for great photographs. One of the advantages of the midnight sun is that you can have landings and get off the ship at any hour. In places like the Ross Sea, where ice and weather can be unpredictable, this allows some expedition operators, such as Heritage Expeditions, to keep exploration schedules flexible. For example, it might be too windy to land at 2pm, but by 9pm it's calm again. You can always sleep later.

FROM LEFT: LIZ CARLSON, DAN LEETH/ALAMY

Focus on Antarctica

FROM EARLY EXPLORERS TO PHOTOGRAPHING ANTARCTICA TODAY

Photography was still relatively new when the Heroic Age of Antarctic exploration (1897–1922) was underway. Many of the more famous expeditions brought a dedicated professional photographer on board, while others had team members bring their own cameras. For many people, their work brought Antarctica – a place seen by few – to life. Their legacy lives on today.

Left Boat from the *Terra Nova* after it ran aground **Centre** Frank Hurley's Debrie Le Parvo camera **Right** The *Endurance* trapped in ice

HERBERT PONTING/ROYAL GEOGRAPHICAL SOCIETY VIA GETTY IMAGES

Some of the most iconic and instantly recognizable photos from Antarctica were taken during the Heroic Age. Like the ghostly silhouette of the *Endurance* ship trapped in the ice under a black winter night. Or the *Terra Nova* ship photographed from the inside of an ice cave. Or who can forget the sled dog puppies? Photography went hand in hand with the diaries, detailing the stories of survival and hardship, and was often an important part of the expedition. Often, explorers like Shackleton and Scott would leverage exclusive stories to media outlets to secure sponsorship money for their expensive expeditions in advance. This also included photos and videos, which would later be used for books and on lecture tours.

Capturing Antarctica's First Images

Antarctica's weather conditions can make photography challenging. Wet, windy and wild, it's not a place known for flat seas and blue skies. But if photography in Antarctica is difficult today, imagine what it was like a century ago.

Heroic Age photographers used large wooden plate cameras with glass negatives for high-quality images, hand-cranked motion picture cameras for early films, and smaller folding Kodak cameras for sledging journeys. The cameras were very heavy, and the glass plates were very fragile and could crack in the cold. They used improvised dark rooms, and the chemicals used to develop the images could freeze and were toxic. Some historians have proposed that fumes from the photographic chemicals Frederick Cook used while developing images aboard the poorly ventilated *Belgica* may have exacerbated the crew's

NATIONAL MUSEUM OF AUSTRALIA/

FRANK HURLEY/SCOTT POLAR RESEARCH INSTITUTE, UNIVERSITY OF CAMBRIDGE/GETTY IMAGES

health problems and psychological stress, an ironic possibility given that Cook also served as the expedition's doctor. These cameras produced remarkably detailed images but were heavy, fragile and difficult to operate in extreme Antarctic cold.

Photography Guides

Most expeditions to Antarctica will have a photographer to help capture the trip for everyone. Sometimes they will also serve as photo guides, or there will be separate photo guides, giving advice to passengers about how to take great photos on their trips. Certain trips have photography programs you can sign up for in advance.

> Heroic Age photographers used large wooden plate cameras with glass negatives for high-quality images, hand-cranked motion picture cameras for early films, and smaller folding Kodak cameras for sledging journeys.

Look for Movement

Photographing wildlife at the scale found in Antarctica is overwhelming. Faced with thousands of penguins, it's tempting to shoot everywhere and everything. With wildlife, it pays to be patient and wait for the animal to do something interesting, like a penguin throwing its head back in an ecstatic display or waiting for a chick to pop its head to be fed. Humpback whales on the surface will often show more of their back as they prepare to dive and display the perfect tail fluke.

Herbert Ponting

Herbert Ponting joined Robert Falcon Scott on his *Terra Nova* expedition (1910–13) as the photographer. He managed to shoot more than 1700 glass negatives and over 7.6km of film. One morning at Cape Evans, Ponting was filming a pod of orcas when all of a sudden they began breaking up the ice beneath him. With the orca in pursuit, he ran as fast as he could across the broken ice to the ship, where Scott declared, 'By God, that was about the closest squeak I ever saw.' Ponting later published *The Great White South* in 1921 and produced two films, *The Great White Silence* and *Ninety Degrees South*.

Bright Snow & Ice

If you're lucky and have a bright sunny day, shooting the ice and snow can be tricky. Your camera may try to underexpose the photo, making it grey. If this happens, you might need to manually increase your exposure to compensate for the snow's brightness. And if you're hit with grey, overcast days, don't worry. Darker skies help make blue ice pop out in photos, looking all the brighter.

The Right Gear

If you're new to photography or have invested in new gear before an expedition, make sure you spend some time at home to get to know the ins and outs. You don't want to be figuring out a setting with a breaching whale in front of you. Speaking of breaching whales, wildlife tends to dominate trips to the Peninsula, so make sure you have fast, professional memory cards that can keep up when you're shooting fast-moving wildlife. If you're keeping it to just a smartphone, make sure you have a cord attachment or phone grip on the case for when you're in the Zodiacs.

Wildlife tends to dominate trips to the Peninsula, so make sure you have fast, professional memory cards that can keep up when you're shooting fast-moving wildlife.

Choosing Your Lenses

If you're in a wildlife-dense area of Antarctica, you'll want to have a telephoto lens with you, ideally one that reaches around 400mm or longer. For landscapes and icebergs, you'll want a wide-angle lens, at least 24mm or wider.

Wet-Weather Coverage

There can be rain, sleet or snow at any time of day or year in Antarctica, so you should always bring waterproof sleeves, rain covers and even lens hoods. Filters for your lenses are another great way to add a layer of protection.

Even when there is no precipitation, Zodiac rides can get splashy. Make sure everything is in a dry bag or waterproof camera bag. Pro tip: test your waterproof gear at home. Some camera backpacks that are marketed as waterproof aren't Antarctica waterproof. If you get seawater on your gear, make sure you clean it off once you're back onboard to prevent salt corrosion.

FRANK HURLEY/WIKIMEDIA/PUBLIC DOMAIN, COURTESY OF THE MITCHELL LIBRARY, STATE LIBRARY OF NEW SOUTH WALES

UNIVERSITY OF CAMBRIDGE/GETTY IMAGES

HERBERT PONTING/ROYAL GEOGRAPHICAL SOCIETY VIA GETTY IMAGES

HERBERT PONTING/WIKIMEDIA/PUBLIC DOMAIN

Condensation

The drastic temperature change between the ship and the elements can cause moisture buildup in your equipment. Consider bringing moisture-absorbent pads to place throughout your gear, or leave it in a sealed bag to slowly warm up once you're back onboard.

Backup Gear

Always carry plenty of backup gear. If you can afford to, bring multiple camera bodies in case one has issues. You can also carry two cameras with different lenses, reducing the need to change lenses out in the field, which can be tricky in bad weather. Make sure you have enough card space to store the photos you'll take (you'll have thousands of penguins) and multiple batteries. Batteries drain much faster in the cold, and you might need more than one on a single outing.

Insurance

Before traveling south, make sure you have good insurance for your equipment and that it covers you when you're abroad. It's much better to pay the deductible than to replace a camera.

Frank Hurley

Perhaps the most famous of all of the expedition photographers accompanying Shackleton on his *Endurance* expedition, Frank Hurley actually got his start on Douglas Mawson's Australasian Antarctic Expedition (1911–14). A year after departing Antarctica, he returned to the Weddell Sea with Shackleton. His photos of the *Endurance* trapped in the sea ice are iconic, and he was known for experimenting by making composite images or taking an hour-long exposure at night. When the *Endurance* began to sink beneath the ice, Hurley had to choose the best of his negatives to bring with him, smashing the rest so he wouldn't be tempted to sneak them along.

From far left to right Adélie penguin by Frank Hurley; Seals on pancake ice off Cape Evans by Herbert Ponting; Penguins at Cape Royds by Herbert Ponting; View of the *Terra Nova* from inside an iceberg cave by Herbert Ponting

27 Science in ACTION

RESEARCH | LEARNING | CITIZEN SCIENCE

Under the 1959 Antarctic Treaty, Antarctica is reserved for peaceful purposes, scientific research and environmental protection. Today it produces leading research across climate science, ice dynamics, oceanography, wildlife biology, microbiology, astronomy and physics. Many expedition guides have worked at Antarctic research stations, bringing firsthand experience to the table.

How to

Access Visiting scientific stations is free but it is intermittent and ad hoc, depending on approval and logistics.

Ship help Expedition ships often support research stations by transporting staff and supplies.

Empty bases Many bases were built and occupied across Antarctica in the 1950s, motivated by the International Geophysical Year (1957–58) to support coordinated scientific research. Many were later abandoned, but can still be visited today.

Scientific Support

Research stations Four principal research stations operate in the Ross Sea region: **McMurdo Station** (USA), **Scott Base** (New Zealand), **Jang Bogo Station** (South Korea) and **Mario Zucchelli Station** (Italy, summer only). Together they support research on climate, glaciology, marine ecosystems, volcanology, astrophysics, mapping and the upper atmosphere.

Citizen science Many expedition ships offer opportunities for passengers to participate in citizen science. Guests can submit humpback whale tail photos to Happywhale (happywhale.com), which uses AI photo identification to track individual whales and migration patterns. Seabird surveys during crossings often contribute to eBird (ebird.org), the Cornell Lab of Ornithology's global database. Heritage Expeditions guests have assisted researchers in collecting ancient penguin

Work Your Way to Antarctica

Research stations You don't have to be a scientist to work at a station. Check if your country operates an Antarctic research station. Many nations run bases across the continent and hire staff to support science, logistics and daily operations.

Hiring cycles Learn when recruitment happens. Antarctic programs hire far in advance – application timelines are important.

Relevant experience Highlight experience in remote locations, outdoor work or expedition environments.

Medical clearance Ensure you can pass a comprehensive medical assessment.

Persistence Be patient and persistent. It can take years to land your first job.

Matty Jordan, *Antarctic project manager and science communicator. @mattykjordan*

bones for paleoecology studies.

Dry Valleys Scientists believe the Dry Valleys are the closest terrestrial equivalent to Mars' terrain. Huge and desolate, these snow-free valleys in the Transantarctic Mountains hold some of the world's most extraordinary living forms. Despite the oft-quoted statement that no rain has fallen there for at least two million years, it has indeed rained in the **McMurdo Dry Valleys** (including in 1959, 1968, 1970 and 1974). The valleys are also known for eerie mummified seals that wandered inland long ago and were preserved by the extreme cold and dryness. Scenic offers helicopter flights (additional cost) to the Dry Valleys if weather permits.

Above McMurdo Dry Valleys

SEABIRDS

01 Wilson's storm petrel
Tiny seabirds nicknamed 'Jesus birds' for their appearance of walking on water (hovering while feeding). They are considered one of the most abundant seabirds.

02 Southern royal albatross
With a wingspan over 3m, they are long-lived and slow to reproduce.

03 Antarctic petrel
Dark brown and white petrels are frequently seen soaring above the ice, and it breeds only on the Antarctic continent.

04 Hoiho/yellow-eyed penguin
The rarest penguin in the world prefers to nest in the scrub and is endemic to New Zealand and the subantarctic.

05 Sooty shearwater
Dark brown seabird that flies low over the waves and travels for thousands of miles.

06 Adélie penguin
With a bright white ring around their eyes, they can be found in huge colonies in the Antarctic.

07 Snow petrel
Soaring above the pack ice, their all-white plumage is unmistakable.

08 Light-mantled albatross
Beautiful with sleek, dark plumage and pale eyes, they're easy to spot, especially when they follow ships.

09 Rockhopper penguin
Of the three subspecies of this crested penguin, the eastern species is the most commonly seen in New Zealand and the Australian subantarctic.

10 Emperor penguin
The largest penguin breeds in winter on the sea ice and has the deepest and longest dives known of any bird.

11 Royal penguin
Breeding on Macquarie Island and found around the subantarctic, their white face and yellow feathers make them stand out.

12 Antarctic prion
Ranging throughout the Southern Ocean, these small grey-blue birds fly low over the waves.

13 Kelp gull
The only gull of the Southern Ocean, they are opportunistic feeders and are very widespread.

28 Subantarctic BIRDLIFE

SEABIRDS | PENGUINS | NATURE

New Zealand maintains five subantarctic island groups as both National Nature Reserves and UNESCO World Heritage Sites. Remote, unoccupied and hard to get to, these islands teem with wildlife. Ships heading to the Ross Sea from New Zealand and Australia often visit these islands.

LIZ CARLSON

How to

All the birds Ten species of penguin have been recorded, and four species breed here regularly. Ten species of albatross breed in the region (five breed nowhere else).

Trip duration Pay close attention to the length of trips; an ideal length would be 30 days, but devoted birdwatchers might want longer.

Management The subantarctic islands are managed as national nature reserves by the Department of Conservation (DOC; doc.govt.nz) and all landings require permits.

NATURE PICTURE LIBRARY/ALAMY

Rare Penguins on the Snares Islands

Discovered by accident, the **Snares Islands** are the closest subantarctic islands to New Zealand. With no human settlement and no invasive mammal populations, the native species here have thrived unlike anywhere else. Known as Māori Tini Heke, it earned its English name as sailors considered the Snares a shipping hazard. Snares crested penguins only breed here. It is very protected and there are no landings here; you can only visit by ship or Zodiac cruise.

RICHARD MCMANUS/GETTY IMAGES

Heritage & History on the Auckland Islands

The largest of New Zealand's subantarctic islands are 465km south of the South Island: the **Auckland Islands**. This is a birder's

Other Subantarctic Islands

Repositioning voyages by Ponant, Hapag-Lloyd, Aurora Expeditions and others between Australia, New Zealand and Ushuaia may attempt to visit the **Balleny Islands** or **Peter I Island**. **Tristan da Cunha** sees occasional cruise calls, while **Kerguelen**, **Crozet** and **Amsterdam** are reached by rare passenger berths on resupply vessels.

Above left Snares crested penguins, Snares Islands **Left** Antipodes Islands (p175) **Above** Bounty Island shag, near Bounty Islands (p175)

wonderland with 38 native bird species, 25 of which breed nowhere else, and nine of which are found nowhere else on Earth. Most operators call in at **Enderby Island**, a predator-free paradise of albatross, penguins and sea lions.

The islands hold deep cultural and spiritual significance for Ngāi Tahu, the principal Māori *iwi* (tribe) of the South Island. Oral traditions describe early Māori voyages to the Auckland Islands to gather food and other resources.

Predator-Free Campbell Island

The most southerly of New Zealand's subantarctic islands, **Campbell Island** is a biodiversity haven. Rich in wildlife and history, it was once used by farmers, sealers and whalers. The island was decimated by the introduction of rats, feral cats, sheep and cattle, all of which were successfully removed in 2006.

It's famous for its megaherbs, oversized herbaceous wildflowers with large leaves and colorful blooms, which blanket the island in

Restoring Maukahuka/Auckland Island

Over the past 200 years, introduced pests such as goats, cattle, rabbits, pigs, cats and mice have caused severe ecological damage to the Auckland Islands, killing seabirds, eating eggs and damaging native plants. Today, **Maukahuka/Auckland Island** (the largest island in the group) is the only subantarctic island that still has mammalian pests. A partnership between the indigenous tribe Ngāi Tahu, DOC, NZ Nature Fund and other groups aims to remove the pests through the NZ$80 million Maukahuka Restoration Project, one of the largest pest eradication efforts ever attempted. If successful, it will restore 46,000 hectares of habitat and allow seabirds and native wildlife to recover.

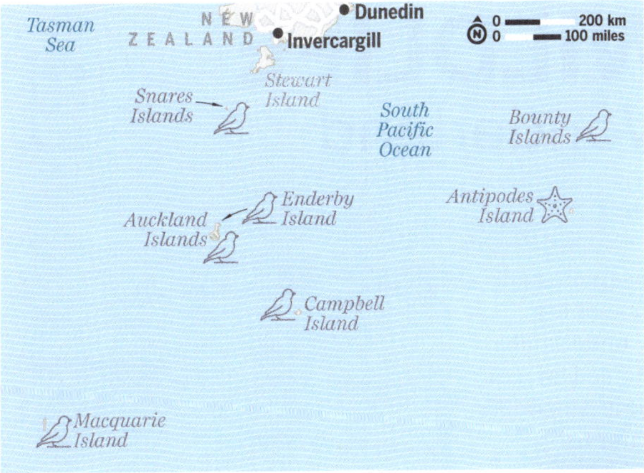

summer. Their size is an adaptation to the relentless wind, cold and exposure.

The Isolated Antipodes Islands

The **Antipodes Islands** are volcanic in origin and lie over 800 km south of New Zealand. Rugged and exposed with steep sea cliffs, they are not often visited. Home to unique wildlife, it's hard to imagine that once all the seals here were hunted to extinction. In the 19th century, ships regularly crossed these treacherous subantarctic waters, and castaway depots were established to support potential shipwreck survivors, one of which can still be seen today. In 2018, all mice had been eradicated from the Antipodes, making it officially pest-free and allowing wildlife to thrive once more.

Wild & Windswept Bounty Islands

Once you hit the roaring forties, the nickname for the windy area between 40° and 50° South, you'll understand why wind-loving birds like albatross thrive here. The **Bounty Islands** were sighted and named in 1788 by Captain William Bligh of HMS *Bounty*, which would later be the star of the most famous mutiny in history. Wild, windy, rocky and harsh, it has an appeal of its own, with many unique birds nesting here – like the Bounty Island shag and erect-crested penguins.

Left Maukahuka/Auckland Island vegetation **Below** Southern royal albatross, Enderby Island

FROM LEFT: CINDY HOPKINS/ALAMY, WOLFGANG KAEHLER/LIGHTROCKET VIA GETTY IMAGES

29 WILDLIFE Wonderland

WILDLIFE | HISTORY | SCIENCE

Halfway between Tasmania and continental Antarctica is one of the most biologically diverse wonderlands: **Macquarie Island**. Nicknamed 'Macca,' this little 34km-long island is Australia's answer to South Georgia, and its leading attractions are the immense wildlife colonies. It's the only place on Earth where rocks from the mantle, 6km below the ocean floor, are actively exposed above sea level.

How to

Entry It's part of Australia and you need a passport to visit. If you're not from New Zealand or Australia, you'll need an Australian visa.

When to go January and February are when chicks are born. Heritage Expeditions runs trips to the sub-antarctic islands from November to December. Most expeditions to the Ross Sea include stops here.

Wildlife density There are 100,000 seals and 4 million penguins, including 150,000 king penguin breeding pairs. Bring a telephoto lens.

Royal penguins One of the biggest drawcards of Macquarie Island is seeing royal penguins, which can only be found here (there are 850,000 breeding pairs). **Sandy Bay** is a wildlife stronghold, home to thousands of penguins and seals and featuring a lush, mountainous backdrop. There is a nice boardwalk up to a viewpoint over the royal penguin colony, while the king colony sits at the other end of the beach.

King penguins After the sealing era ended, ships returned here and killed king and royal penguins for their oil. Visiting now, you see so many of the populations bouncing back. **Lusitania Bay** is home to one of the largest king penguin colonies in the world, with up to half a million birds. On a Zodiac cruise along the shoreline, you can get a feel for the scale and density of wildlife.

ROBERT HARDING VIDEO/SHUTTERSTOCK

For those seeking photos of king penguins packed tightly together, this is your spot.

Science In 1948, a scientific station was established by ANARE (Australian National Antarctic Research Expeditions) at the Isthmus on the site occupied by Douglas Mawson's men in 1911. Between 14 and 40 people work at **Macquarie Island Station** at any given time. Tucked on the Isthmus, a 500m-wide scrap of land between Buckles Bay and Garden Cove, you'll find the base surrounded by penguins and seals.

Mawson's Macquarie Island

When famed Australian geologist and explorer Douglas Mawson landed a scientific party here during his Australasian Antarctic Expedition (1911–14), he was met by the crew of the *Clyde*, shipwrecked a month earlier, who were prepared to defend their sealing rights against what they initially thought were rival sealers. Once the mix-up was straightened out, the party Mawson left on the island used a wireless relay station set up on **Wireless Hill** in the first two-way communication between Australia and Antarctica. Impressed by the island, Mawson returned to Australia advocating protection against the widespread exploitation here, which led to it becoming a wildlife sanctuary in 1933.

Above King penguin colony, Macquarie Island

EAST ANTARCTICA & THE SOUTH POLE

EXPLORATION | WILDLIFE | POLAR

RESEARCHED BY LIZ CARLSON

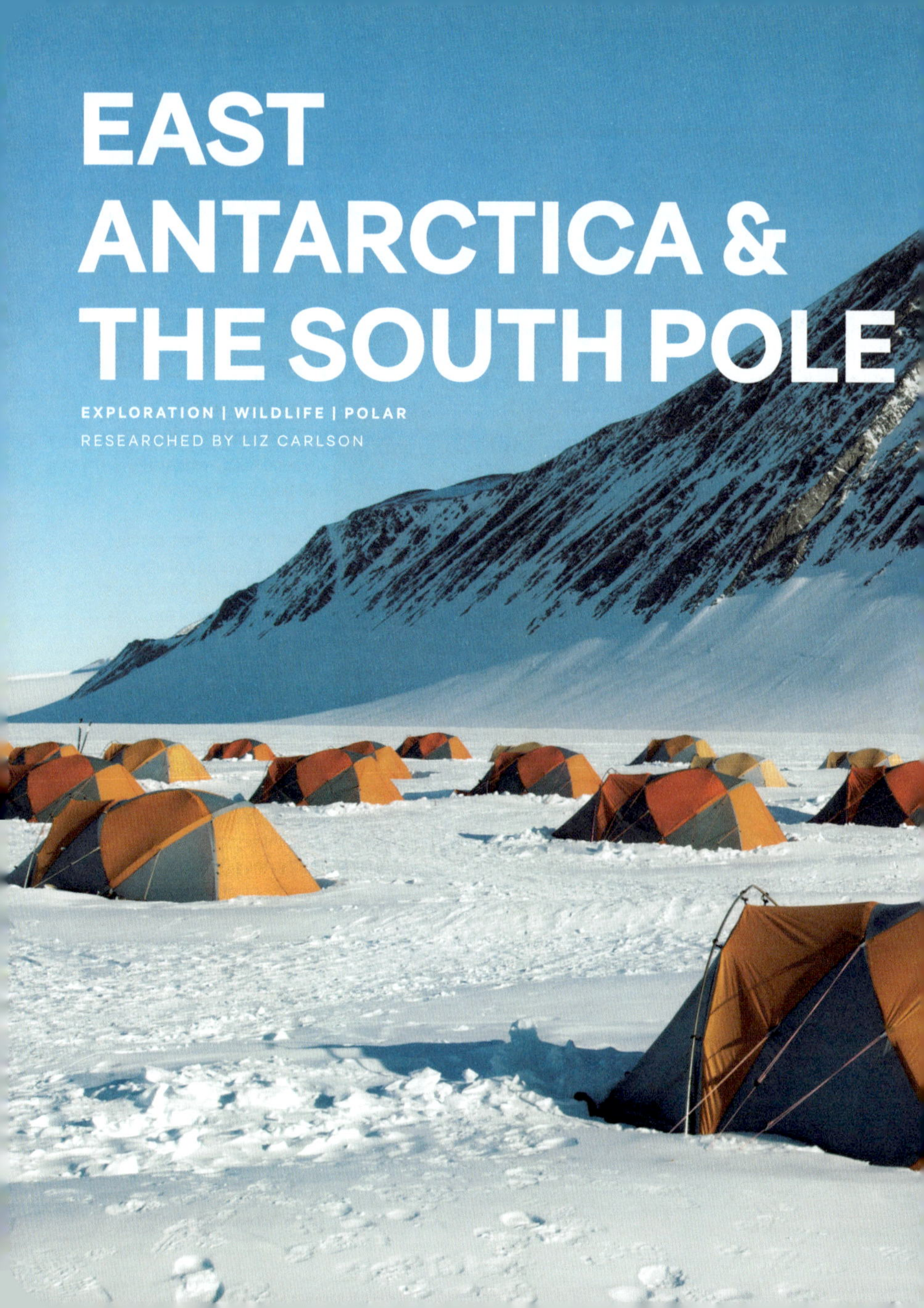

EAST ANTARCTICA & THE SOUTH POLE

Trip Builder

Less than 1% of Antarctic visitors travel to East Antarctica, the South Pole, and the continent's interior, compared with 116,000 who visit the Antarctic Peninsula each year. Vast and extreme, this region includes Antarctica's coldest temperatures, rare ice-free oases and teeming emperor penguin colonies.

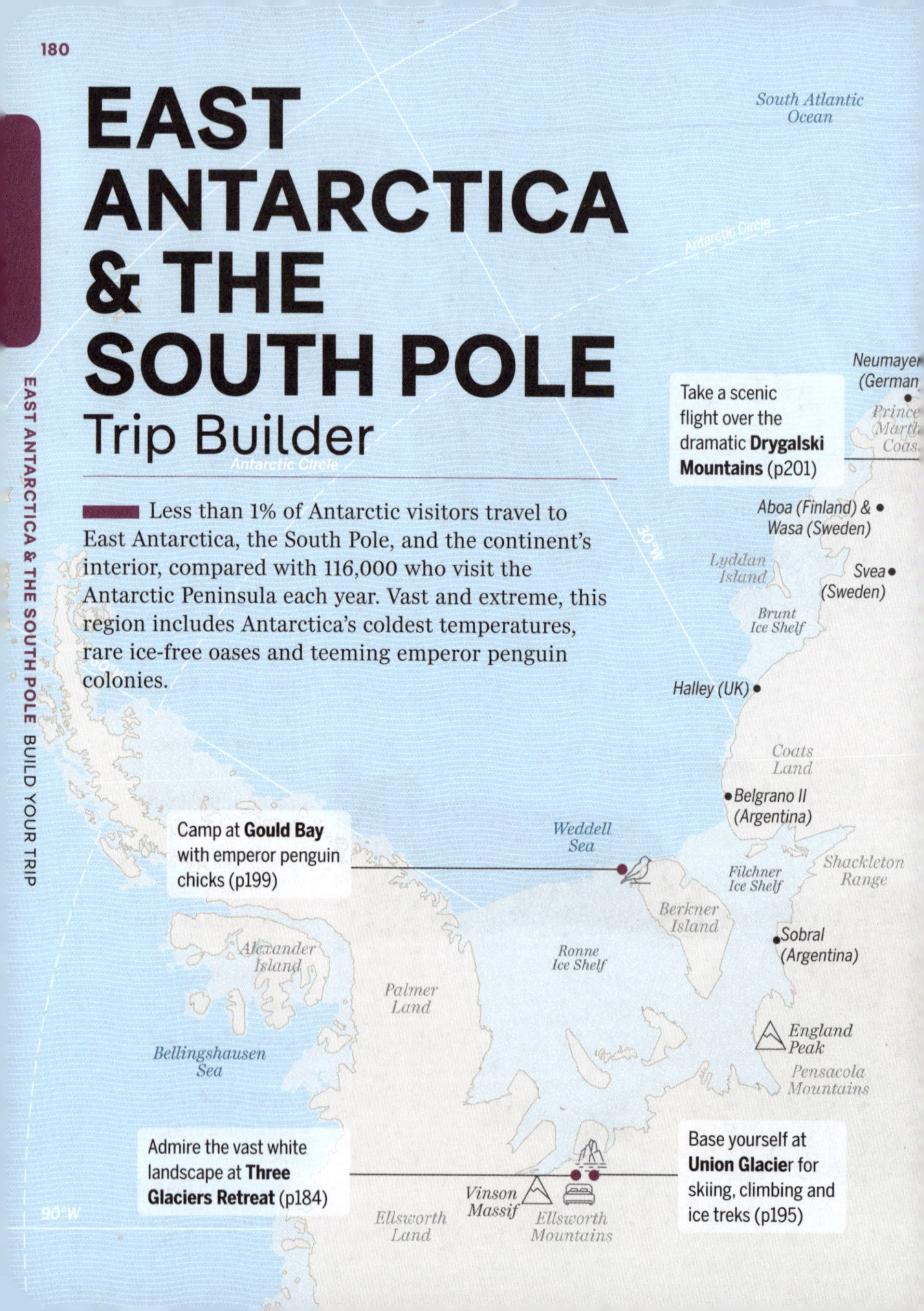

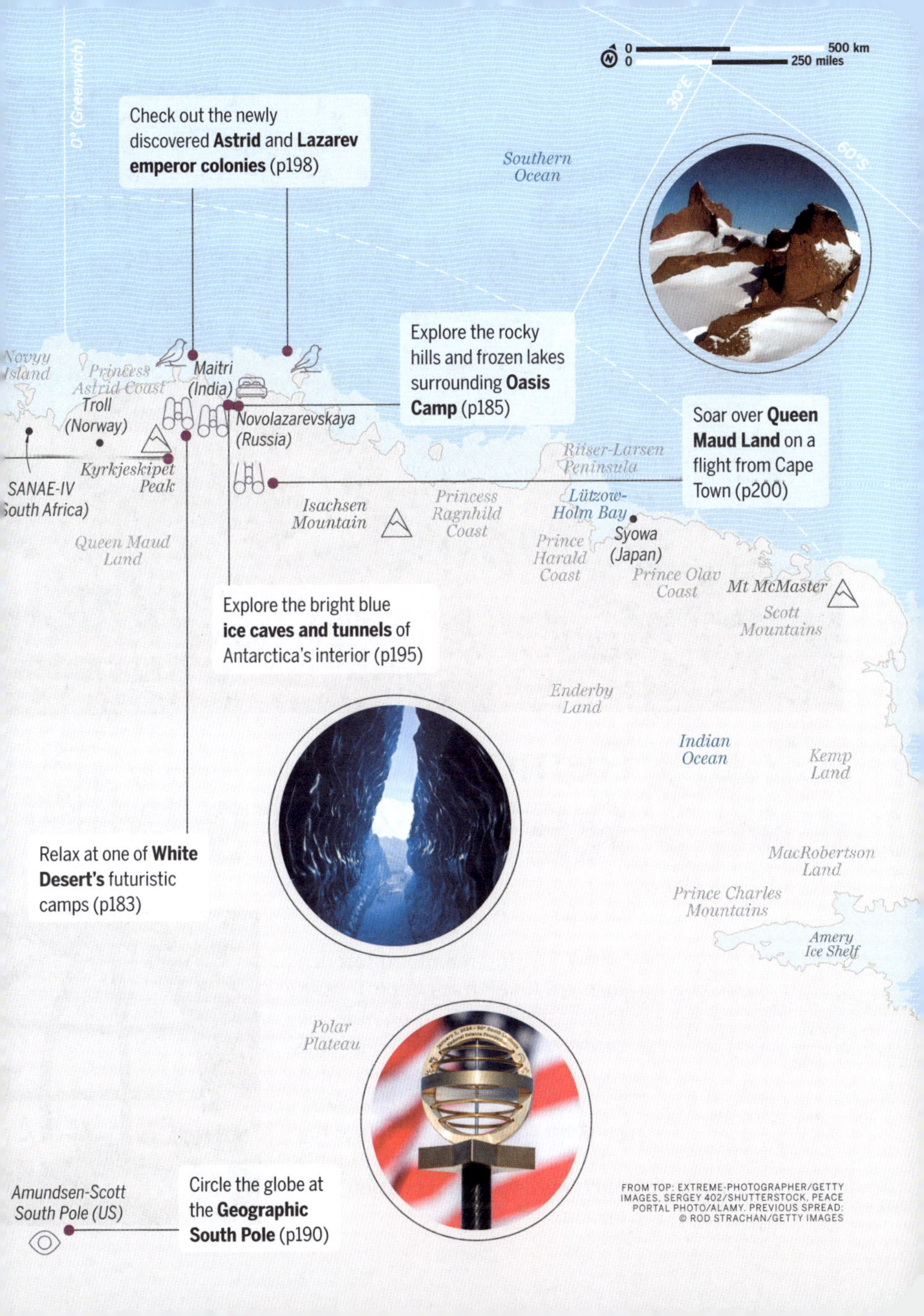

FROM TOP: EXTREME-PHOTOGRAPHER/GETTY IMAGES, SERGEY 402/SHUTTERSTOCK, PEACE PORTAL PHOTO/ALAMY. PREVIOUS SPREAD: © ROD STRACHAN/GETTY IMAGES

30 Remote Ice RETREATS

LUXURY | PRIVATE | SCENERY

Visiting remote Antarctica involves flying from Cape Town or Punta Arenas to land on blue ice runways. Three operators run base camps where visitors can travel to the South Pole, see emperor penguin colonies and explore the interior. These are the continent's only tourist accommodation options.

COURTESY OF WHITE DESERT

Upscale Lodgings at Whichaway Camp

Glamping doesn't seem to be a strong enough word to convey the majesty of **Whichaway Camp**, White Desert's first camp. It sits amid exposed rock, glacier ice and more than 100 freshwater lakes. Today, six state-of-the-art pods with an old-world-exploration vibe rest on the rocky terrain, each with a private bathroom and a glass conservatory overlooking the glacial landscape; they host up to 12 guests. Designed to feel incredibly comfortable in one of the most isolated places on Earth, White Desert is the definition of luxury.

Sleep in Futuristic Pods

White Desert's **Echo Base** feels less like glamping off-grid and more like a luxury camp on Mars. Tucked deep in Queen Maud Land, a

How to

Getting here There are three operators. White Desert (white-desert.com) and Ultima Antarctica Expeditions (ultima-antarcticexpeditions.com) fly in from Cape Town, South Africa. Antarctic Logistics & Expeditions (ALE; antarctic-logistics.com) flies in from Punta Arenas, Chile.

When to go Late October to early February.

Cost and duration Most trips are under a week (prices start at US$25,000 but average around US$70,000–80,000). Flight timings are dictated by weather conditions, so itineraries can shift. Extra buffer time is essential.

Above left Whichaway Camp
Below left Pod, Echo Base

remote stretch of East Antarctica claimed by Norway, it's surrounded by jagged black rock and endless glaciers – so stark and otherworldly. Inspired by astronaut Buzz Aldrin's visit, these futuristic pods can host up to 12 and are warm, quiet and unexpectedly plush, with big windows that make the landscape feel like part of the room. It's the kind of place where you sip a perfectly made cocktail while staring out at pure wilderness, and have to remind yourself you're still on Earth.

Quiet Base at Three Glaciers Retreat

A 15-minute flight away from ALE's Union Glacier Camp is the exclusive **Three Glaciers Retreat**. Tucked away in the Ellsworth Mountains, it can accommodate 16 guests at a time. A bespoke, cozy base with spacious heated polar tents with all the trimmings, you can gaze at the surrounding glaciers from your patio. It offers a streamlined experience and it's a more refined alternative to Union Glacier for inland activities. Closer to the

Supporting Science

All three operators support scientific research in Antarctica by transporting scientists, staff and equipment to remote field sites across the continent, as well as providing search-and-rescue support. About half of White Desert's logistics operations support science, including grants for projects such as studying Antarctic meteorites and the microbial life associated with them. ALE assists research initiatives such as POLENET (polenet.org), which monitors movement within the Antarctic ice sheet. Ultima supports studies of microorganisms in the ice-covered Lake Untersee and provides logistical assistance to a range of National Antarctic Programmes (NAP; omnap.aq).

Blue Ice Runways

Have you ever wondered how planes land in Antarctica? The answer is blue ice runways. Glacial ice is much harder and denser than snow, allowing large aircraft to land on the solid surface. In parts of interior Antarctica, more snow is removed by strong winds than falls; this exposes glacier ice that can be shaped into natural runways.

South Pole than other camps, you can fly there and back without a fuel stop.

Oasis Camp's Luxury Cabins

A 30-minute drive (yes, there are vehicles in Antarctica) from their local airstrip will bring you to Ultima's **Oasis Camp**, a series of stylish wooden cabins where you can base yourself on an adventure around Queen Maud Land. Hosting up to 20 guests, the camp faces east, overlooking a sheltered ice valley and a pristine lake, framed by rocky nunataks (p201). There is even a traditional *banya* (sauna) on site. Meals are taken together in the lounge and dining cabin, where a dedicated chef prepares hearty dishes.

Glamping on the Ice

Explorer Camp feels like White Desert's nod to classic expedition travel. Set beneath the jagged T-Rex Mountain, this spot sits on open ice, with nothing softening the landscape's scale. The setup is still high-end but deliberately closer to the elements, with heated tents rather than pods, communal meals and shared showers. Of White Desert's three camps, this is the most pared-back and rustic, though it's still luxurious by Antarctic standards.

Far left & top right Three Glaciers Retreat **Bottom right** Explorer Camp

31 INTERIOR Activities

HIKING | SKIING | BIKING

In addition to the main features of a trip to interior Antarctica, like emperor penguins or the South Pole, the camps have a wide range of activities you can take part in every day. Exploration options here are extensive, and expert guides are on hand to offer options based on weather and conditions. Take your pick.

COURTESY OF WHITE DESERT

How to

Activities Along with standard activities, some camps offer abseiling, ziplining, snowshoeing and snowmobiling. ALE offers skydiving.

Small groups Most camps accommodate a small number of guests at a time, allowing excursions to be flexible and tailored to the group.

Guides All camps have highly experienced mountain guides who organize activities, and assess conditions and weather.

Gear Check with your operator whether you need to buy or rent gear.

SANDIE KESTELL/LONELY PLANET

SANDIE KESTELL/LONELY PLANET

Clockwise from bottom left Fat-tire biking; Exploring icy landscapes; Mountaineering near Three Glaciers Retreat (p184)

Hiking Getting out on your own two feet varies slightly by operator, but it involves exploring icy landscapes that change day by day. The intensity or distance depends on the guests and can be tailored accordingly. White Desert and Ultima offer hikes for all levels, from scenic, viewpoint-focused and accessible exploration to more challenging terrain. ALE leans more towards expeditions, with longer, purpose-focused hikes that can feel more remote and physically demanding, especially on mountaineering departures.

Fat-tire biking Something you might be surprised to see in Antarctica is bikes. Ice terrain can be flat and smooth in places, with 'roads' used by transport vehicles, which make biking possible. Fat biking is offered on some trips with White Desert, ALE and Ultima, depending on conditions. Using specialized bikes with oversized tires, guests can ride across firm snow or hard blue-ice surfaces near the camp (when conditions allow).

Skiing All three operators offer skiing, but in very different ways. With White Desert and Ultima, it tends to be guided outings near camp: non-technical and focused on gliding across firm snow for the experience, rather than covering serious distance. ALE, in addition to offering ski trails and options to ski down local mountains, also supports full expedition-style skiing, including trips from the edge of the continent to the South Pole, or even the last degree to the Pole, where guests haul sleds and travel long distances across the plateau.

Marathons on the Ice

Several marathons take place in Antarctica for runners hoping to tick off a race on all seven continents. At **Union Glacier**, the Antarctic Ice Marathon is held each December, with participants staying at a field camp and running on glacier ice at about 900m elevation in temperatures around -20°C (-4°F) and strong katabatic winds. In East Antarctica, Ultima hosts endurance events, including the Antarctic Ice Ultra, with distances ranging from a half-marathon to 100 miles around the Schirmacher Oasis, as well as the Antarctic leg of the World Marathon Challenge: seven marathons on seven continents in seven days.

32 Stand at 90° SOUTH

WHITE | COLD | VAST

The South Pole is a place of extremes: high altitude, intense cold and very low humidity. The sun stays above the horizon for months before disappearing into months of darkness. Today, visitors can reach it – though the cost is high, and most stay only a few hours.

LEFT: GALEN ROWELL/GETTY IMAGES. RIGHT: PEACE PORTAL PHOTO/ALAMY

How to

Fitness At 2835m above sea level, it feels even higher thanks to atmospheric pressure. Average summer temperatures sit around -25°C (-13°F). Operators generally require a good level of health to visit.

Research base The USA maintains a scientific base at the South Pole. Access to the actual research station is limited, and subject to staff availability and permissions.

Visitor numbers Less than 500 people visit the South Pole per year.

Fly to the South Pole

The Pole itself is among the most isolated spots on Earth, surrounded by thousands of square kilometers unrelieved by a single feature. In every direction you look, there is only an unbroken horizon. There are two ways to get to the South Pole as a tourist: flying or skiing (p191).

All three operators (ALE, Ultima and White Desert) offer day trips to the South Pole, ALE offers an overnight stay. The flight from the base camps to the South Pole is 4½–7 hours, with a stop on the return leg (around 83°) for mandatory pilot rest and refueling, where you rest at a field camp (for White Desert and Ultima). This makes it a long excursion and a big travel day.

PEACE PORTAL PHOTO/ALAMY

Dogsledding in Antarctica

Roald Amundsen reached the South Pole in 1911 using sled dogs, drawing on skills learned from Indigenous Arctic communities. Nearly 100 Greenland dogs pulled Amundsen's sledges up to 30km a day. Dogs were later widely used for Antarctic travel until non-native species were banned. The last dogs were removed in 1994.

Above left Flags at Ceremonial South Pole (p190) **Left** Geographical South Pole marker **Above** White Desert's Basler flight to South Pole

Two South Poles

The iconic photos of the South Pole you've probably seen are of the **Ceremonial South Pole**, which never moves. The flags of the original 12 Antarctic Treaty signatories surround this red-and-white-striped 'barber' pole, capped by a metallic globe, so it offers the perfect photo op. But it's just for show. Not far away is the **Geographic South Pole**, which marks one end of Earth's axis of rotation. It's identified by a steel pole topped with a medallion designed by the previous overwintering crew. Because all lines of longitude meet here, you can walk in a small circle and pass through every time zone in seconds. The ice beneath the Pole shifts about 10m each year, so the marker and the nearby American flag are repositioned annually to keep them at true 90° South.

Other South Poles

In addition to the Geographic and Ceremonial Poles, three other poles are defined in Antarctic geography.

South Magnetic Pole Where a magnetic compass needle points straight down. It drifts northwest about 5–10km each year and is estimated to be at 63.85°S, 135.08°E in 2025.

South Geomagnetic Pole Marks where Earth's magnetic field would lie if it behaved like a perfect dipole magnet centered within the planet. It is estimated at 80.85°S, 107.24°E in 2025.

Pole of Maximum Inaccessibility The point furthest from any Antarctic coastline. It was reached by a Soviet expedition in 1958 and lies at roughly 82°S, 55°E.

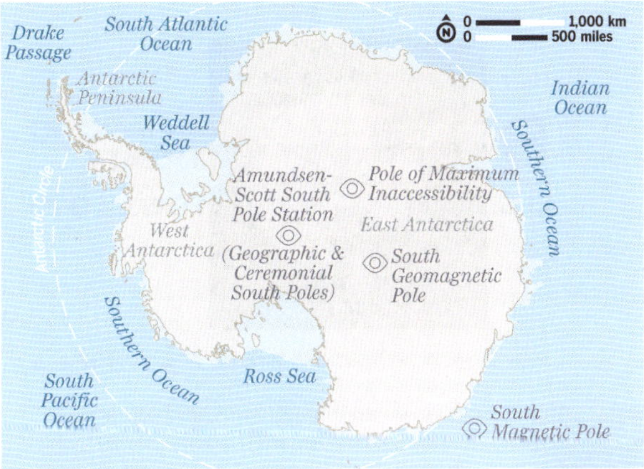

Left Compass needles spinning at the South Magnetic Pole
Below Amundsen–Scott South Pole Station

Ski Your Way South

ALE is the primary deep-field logistics backbone for most commercial South Pole ski expeditions. They operate their own guided ski trips to the South Pole, including flying to 89° South and skiing the last degree to the South Pole, which is 60 nautical miles (111km). You can also ski to the South Pole from other locations further afield in the tracks of the explorers. These trips range from 40 to 60 days, and you must have an extremely high level of fitness, follow a strict training protocol and have skiing experience to undertake them.

View the South Pole Station

Rising above the Antarctic Plateau on stilts, the current **Amundsen–Scott South Pole Station** began full summer operations in 2011. Around 150 people live and work here in summer, dropping to about 50 during the isolated winter. The station supports research in astronomy, auroral science, meteorology, seismology and glaciology, taking advantage of the cold, dry, dark skies at 90° South, free of light pollution and ideal for observing the sky.

Governing Antarctica: The Treaty

ANTARCTICA BELONGS TO NO ONE

Have you ever wondered why there's no passport control in Antarctica? No single country manages it; instead, it's governed cooperatively under the Antarctic Treaty. Treaty countries have agreed that Antarctica will be a peaceful, free and demilitarized zone of international cooperation and scientific research – open to all, with minimal human impact.

Left Antarctic Treaty stamp **Centre** Antarctic Treaty Consultative Meeting, London, 1977 **Right** Turkish science team at work

HOWARD KOSLOW/WIKIMEDIA/PUBLIC DOMAIN

Antarctica is governed through a unique international agreement known as the Antarctic Treaty *(ats.aq)*, which sets aside the continent for peaceful purposes and scientific research. Today, the Treaty has 53 member nations, representing roughly 80% of the world's population. Countries that conduct extensive scientific research in Antarctica can become consultative parties, which gives them the right to participate in decision-making and vote. As a result, Antarctica is often described as a continent belonging to no single nation and managed cooperatively by many.

The International Geophysical Year (1957–58) saw extensive scientific research by 12 countries, which led to the signing of the Treaty. It officially came into force in 1961 and applies to all areas south of 60° S. The agreement established several key principles that still guide Antarctic governance today. It prohibits military activity, ensures freedom for scientific research, promotes international cooperation, and requires countries to share scientific observations and results.

One of the Treaty's most important features is its treatment of land ownership. Seven countries maintain territorial claims in Antarctica (Argentina, Chile, the United Kingdom, Australia, New Zealand, France and Norway). However, the Antarctic Treaty effectively freezes these claims. It neither recognizes nor rejects them, and no new claims can be made while the Treaty is in effect. That being said, several countries have sought to reinforce their sovereignty. These include flagpoles, plaques and stamps, while Argentina has even sent women to the ice to give birth.

FRANK BARRATT/KEYSTONEHULTON ARCHIVE/

SEBNEM COSKUN/ANADOLU VIA GETTY IMAGES

As the years went by, additional agreements were added, known as the Antarctic Treaty System, which strengthened environmental protections and regulated human activity there. One of the biggest additions is the Protocol on Environmental Protection to the Antarctic Treaty, commonly known as the Madrid Protocol, adopted in 1991. This designates Antarctica as a natural reserve devoted to peace and science, establishes strict environmental guidelines for activities on the continent, and prohibits mining and oil drilling (this can be reconsidered in 2048). All new activities must undergo environmental impact assessments.

Marine ecosystems surrounding Antarctica are managed through another agreement, the Commission for the Conservation of Antarctic Marine Living Resources (CCAMLR). Created in 1982, CCAMLR regulates fisheries and protects Antarctic marine ecosystems. In 2016, member nations agreed to establish the world's largest marine protected area in the Ross Sea, protecting more than 1.5 million sq km of ocean.

Tourism and other human activities are also handled under the Antarctic Treaty framework. Countries meet annually at Antarctic Treaty Consultative Meetings to discuss issues such as scientific cooperation, environmental protection, tourism management and the protection of historic sites. Decisions are made by consensus, meaning all consultative members must agree.

Visitor guidelines have also been developed to minimize the environmental impact of tourism. These include site-specific rules at popular landing locations, limits on ship size and visitor numbers at certain sites, and codes of conduct designed to protect wildlife and fragile ecosystems.

The Hot Topic of Krill

Perhaps the biggest issue facing Antarctica today involves one of its smallest animals: krill. Krill are a keystone species in the Southern Ocean, feeding whales, seals and seabirds. Krill fishing remains below quotas, but vessels operate in wildlife-rich areas near the Antarctic Peninsula, prompting scientists to call for stronger protections and better distribution of fishing activity. Fisheries are managed by CCAMLR, which requires consensus. Proposed marine protected areas and updated krill management rules have stalled for years due to objections from Russia and China, who argue that there is not enough scientific evidence to justify the restrictions and that the measures could limit future fishing opportunities.

33 Experience BLUE ICE

LANDSCAPE | LIGHT | PHOTOGRAPHY

A key feature in all of the base camp itineraries is taking in the incredible blue ice of Antarctica's remote interior. While Peninsula trips offer views of glaciers, you rarely get the opportunity to explore tunnels, caves and crevasses surrounded by a blue so bright it has to be seen to be believed.

CHRISTOPHER MICHEL FROM SAN FRANCISCO, USA/WIKIMEDIA/CC BY 2.0

How to

Dry climate Much of Antarctica's interior is technically a desert, receiving very little snowfall each year. Strong winds often scour away loose snow, exposing ancient compressed glacier ice (blue ice).

When to go In some places, ice accessibility depends on the season; some ice melts as the summer progresses.

All ice Around 90% of the world's ice is found here, creating a landscape that is almost entirely frozen.

KATJA RIEDEL / 500PX/GETTY IMAGES

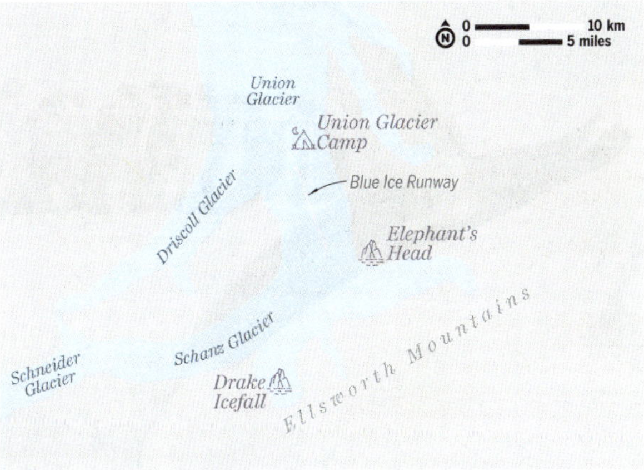

Ice tunnels and caves Many camps sit near ice formations that can be explored when conditions allow. Guided by experts, visitors can descend into tunnels and caves formed within glaciers, where the ice glows neon blue. A short drive from Oasis Camp in the **Schirmacher Oasis** leads to an ice tunnel that can be explored on foot.

Blue river and ice ridges The driscoll is dotted with freshwater lakes. White Desert's 'South Pole & Blue Rivers' trip includes visits to vivid blue meltwater rivers that flow across the tops of glaciers later in the season. Guests can fly over and hike alongside these striking glacial channels near the edge of the continental ice sheet, while trips from **Union Glacier** may visit unique features like the **Drake Icefall**, with ice shaped into large waves.

Crystal caves and freshwater lakes Under certain conditions, temporary caves form where the ice appears like crystals. One such chamber near **Whichaway Camp** glows with shifting light, revealing layers of white and blue. These formations are ephemeral and may appear only briefly early in the season.

Crevasses and glaciers Exploring Antarctica's interior often means walking across ice fields and glaciers in crampons. Near **Oasis Camp**, excursions visit towering ice walls, while ALE's **Union Glacier Camp** sits directly on a glacier, with trips to formations like **Elephant's Head** and opportunities for custom ice climbing.

Above left Drake Icefall
Below left Union Glacier

Ice Cores

When snow falls in Antarctica, it traps tiny amounts of air and atmospheric chemicals. Over time, that snow is compressed into ice, sealing those bubbles inside. By drilling deep ice cores and analyzing the ice and trapped air, scientists can reconstruct past climates. The ratio of oxygen isotopes in the ice reflects the temperatures at the time the snow fell. Some cores, such as those from Vostok and Dome C, extend back hundreds of thousands of years, revealing ice ages and warmer periods. The air bubbles also show past greenhouse gas levels, volcanic eruptions and even human pollution.

34 Emperor Penguin COLONIES

PENGUINS | REMOTE | PHOTOGRAPHY

The only Antarctic bird that breeds in the wintertime is the emperor penguin. They're hard to see in the wild, not because they are rare (population estimates are upwards of 500,000 birds), but because they live in one of the least accessible environments on Earth.

How to

Breeding cycle Emperors breed in the winter, laying an egg in May/June, which the male incubates on its feet beneath a brood patch. They hatch in July or August.

When to go Emperor penguin chicks are out and about in the colonies in their thick grey 'biggles suits' until the end of December or early January, when they begin to fledge.

From space Researchers can find colonies by looking for huge patches of guano from satellites in space.

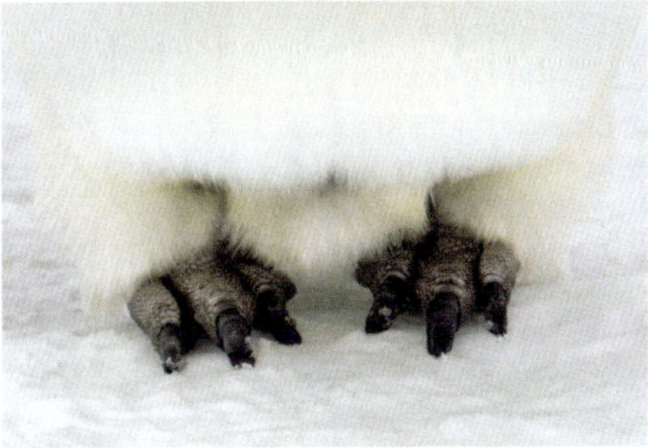

One of Antarctica's Rarest Encounters

Declared endangered by the International Union for Conservation of Nature in April 2026, emperors are the largest species of penguin. They are thought to be found in 66 colonies, only a few of which are accessible to tourists. These are found along the coast of Queen Maud Land and in the Weddell Sea, and you have to fly out to visit them. Aside from visiting the South Pole, an excursion to the emperor colonies is one of the most popular trips in interior Antarctica. While the colonies listed below are the most commonly visited, there are several others in the region that can also be reached, depending on conditions.

You'll likely see individual or groups of emperors on a Ross Sea trip (p158), but they're very rarely seen on the Antarctic Peninsula,

Halley Bay Disappearance

Because they breed on sea ice, emperor penguins are more susceptible to climate and weather events. Halley Bay was the second-largest emperor colony and suffered a catastrophic breeding failure in 2016 when the sea ice broke up before the chicks could fledge. The ice failed to form again in 2017 and 2018, effectively wiping out the colony.

Clockwise from bottom left Emperor penguin colony, Atka Bay (p199); Emperor penguin jumps out of the water; Emperor male penguin incubates an egg

except for specialty trips to Snow Hill (p214). All operators follow the IAATO guidelines at the emperor colonies, from landing the plane far enough away to avoid disturbance to maintaining viewing distances. Visiting the colonies depends on weather and conditions, but all the operators do everything they can to make a visit possible.

Explore Multiple Colonies

The **Astrid Colony** and **Lazarev Colony** were both discovered via satellite imagery. Home to thousands of chicks come springtime, a short flight in a Twin Otter from the Ultima base will bring you there. There are several different colonies that can be visited in the area. You'll get to spend a few hours at the colonies, watching the chicks as they toddle around – something so few ever get to experience. On

Photographing the Emperors

Distance Keeping distance from wildlife is an IAATO requirement, especially around emperor penguin colonies, so bring a telephoto lens for close portraits. A range of 100–400mm (full frame equivalent) works well.

Exposure In bright conditions, slightly overexpose to keep snow looking white. +1 stop is a good starting point, but always check the histogram to avoid clipped highlights.

Temperature On the sea ice near emperor penguins, temperatures can hover around -20°C early in the season. Bring spare batteries and thin gloves that still allow you to operate your camera.

Jarryd Salem, *wildlife photographer and expedition guide. @jarrydsalem*

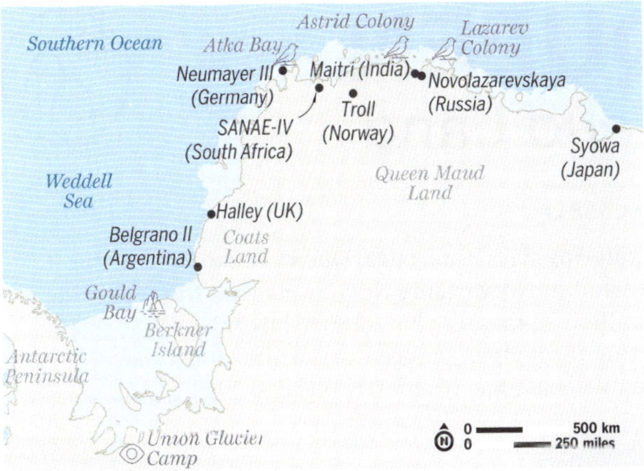

Left Emperor penguins on sea ice
Below Emperor penguin chick, Atka Bay

the 'Emperors and Mountains' trip, you aim to visit two different colonies.

Camp by the Emperors at Gould Bay

ALE offers the only field camp by an emperor penguin colony. This will give you the most time at a colony as you stay multiple days. It's expedition-style, with mountaineering tents set up on the sea ice (gear is provided), and the experience includes a chef. A four-hour flight from **Union Glacier Camp** will bring you to the sea ice at **Gould Bay** (p131); the camp is 2–3km from the colony to minimize disturbance.

A Long-Studied Emperor Colony

A two-hour flight from White Desert's camps will bring you to the fringes of the Weddell Sea. Here you can find one of the larger emperor penguin colonies: **Atka Bay**, where 10,000 breeding pairs of emperor penguins call the ice home. Scientists have been studying them here for decades. The sea ice attaches to the ice shelf (fast ice), offering protection along with polynyas (areas of open water kept ice-free by wind and currents) where they can feed, allowing the colony to thrive. There are other colonies that White Desert can visit as well.

FROM LEFT: SERGEY 402/SHUTTERSTOCK, ROSEMARY CALVERT/GETTY IMAGES

35 QUEEN Maud Land

SCENERY | MOUNTAINS | LANDSCAPE

When it comes to exploring East Antarctica, Queen Maud Land is the gateway ('Dronning Maud Land in Norwegian'; Norway claimed the region in 1939). Spanning nearly 3 million sq km, it's characterized by thick ice sheets and jagged mountains cutting through an endless, dry, white landscape. With high walls of ice along its coastline, it's mostly inaccessible by ship.

WILFRIED BAUER/WIKIMEDIA/CC BY-SA 3.0

How to

Operators Ultima and White Desert are based in Queen Maud Land and have a variety of experiences and activities that explore the region.

Science bases 12 research stations operate here. Belgium's Princess Elisabeth Station was the first zero-emission station in Antarctica.

Norwegian name Queen Maud Land was named in honor of Queen Maud of Norway by the Norwegian explorer Hjalmar Riiser-Larsen during an aerial expedition in 1930.

XTREME-PHOTOGRAPHER/GETTY IMAGES

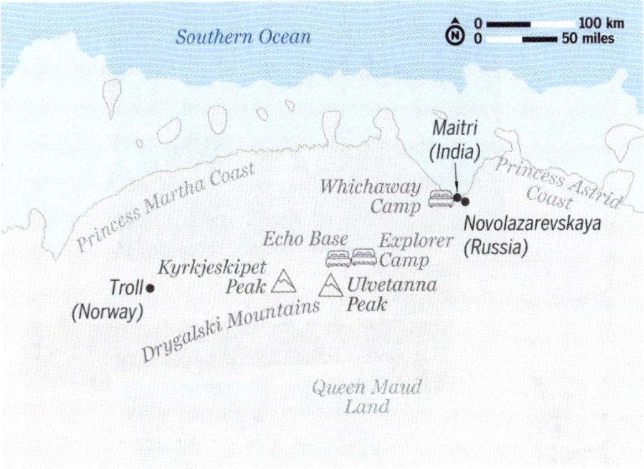

Flying to the Drygalski Mountains Queen Maud Land is one of the least visited parts of Antarctica, seeing only a few hundred tourists each year. One of the best ways to understand its immense scale is from above. Flying into the camps will give you great views over enormous glaciers and huge ice sheets. Dramatic mountains dot the landscape, with the stunning **Drygalski Mountains** on the horizon. Smaller planes on skis, like Twin Otters (small, twin-engine bush planes), can land at multiple spots in these mountains in the same day. **Ulvetanna Peak** juts upwards, the Matterhorn of the Antarctic, beckoning only the boldest (and most well-funded) climbers. The occasional snow petrel might swoop by to have a look. White Desert's runway and **Echo Base** sit in the shadows of these mountains.

Norse mythology Queen Maud Land leans heavily into Norse mythology when it comes to place names, and nowhere is that more obvious than in the Drygalski Mountains. The range is home to Fenriskjeften, or 'The Fenris Jaw,' named for the savage wolf of Norse mythology. Its sharp, tooth-like spires serve as a stark tribute to the monstrous son of Loki. From the air, it makes sense: the seven sharp peaks look like a set of jaws rising out of the ice. At their center sits the plateau Fenristunga, literally 'the wolf's tongue,' surrounded by summits with names like Ulvetanna (wolf's tooth), Kintanna (wolf's molar), Holtanna (hollow tooth) and Mundlauga (mouth).

Above left Drygalski Mountains with Ulvetanna Peak on right **Below left** Holtanna (hollow tooth)

Nunataks: Mountains Beneath the Ice

In Queen Maud Land, scattered rocky summits break through the ice sheet, revealing the highest points of mountain ranges otherwise buried beneath Antarctica's ice. These exposed peaks are called nunataks (from the Greenlandic word 'lonely peak'). Over millions of years, the ice sheet flowed across the continent, submerging most of the landscape. Only the highest ridges and summits remain exposed, standing like islands in a frozen sea. In Queen Maud Land's interior ranges, these rocky outcrops offer rare access to Antarctica's underlying geology and serve as important reference points in an otherwise featureless expanse of ice.

Grace Cordsen, *polar researcher and expedition manager.* @graceforimpact

Types
OF ICE

01 Glacier
A slow-moving river of compressed ice that flows from high accumulation areas toward lower elevations or the sea.

02 Pancake ice
Circular pieces of new sea ice with raised edges are formed as waves bump and freeze slushy ice together.

03 Icebergs
Huge chunks of freshwater ice that calve from glaciers or ice shelves and float in the ocean.

04 Grease ice
A very thin layer of freshly formed sea ice that gives the ocean surface a matte appearance.

05 Tabular iceberg
A flat-topped, steep-sided iceberg that calves from ice shelves, often stretching for kilometers across the sea.

06

07

08

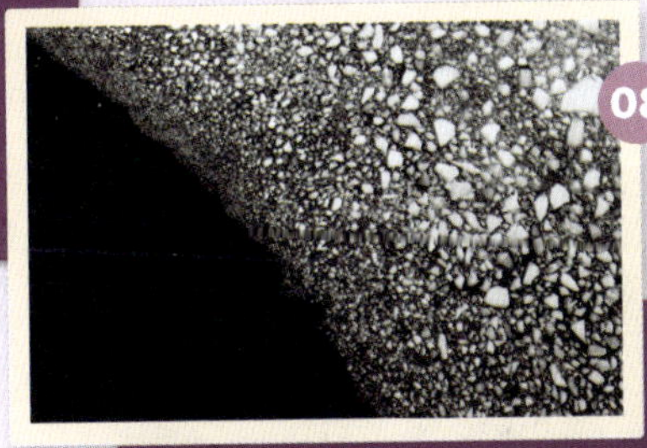

09

10

06 Crevasse
A deep crack or fracture in a glacier forms as the ice stretches and moves over uneven terrain.

07 Pack ice
This is sea ice that forms on the surface of the water, compressing together and constantly moving; sometimes it doesn't melt in summer, leading to multi-year pack ice.

08 Brash ice
Small, broken fragments of floating ice are often churned together between larger ice floes or around ships.

09 Flipped iceberg
An iceberg that has rolled over, revealing the shiny, bright blue ice that was once underwater.

10 Ice shelf
A thick, floating extension of land-based glacier ice, attached to the continent that juts out and sits on ocean water.

01 OLEKSANDR MATSIBURA/SHUTTERSTOCK, 02 IAMCAUSE/SHUTTERSTOCK, 03 YANDONG YANG/SHUTTERSTOCK, 04 MALCOLM SCHUYL/ALAMY, 05 ALEXEY SEAFARER/SHUTTERSTOCK, 06 HOLGER LEUE/GETTY IMAGES, 07 KARENFOLEYPHOTOGRAPHY/SHUTTERSTOCK, 08 MIOLMOR/SHUTTERSTOCK, 09 ALISON WRIGHT/ALAMY, 10 VARGAJONES/GETTY IMAGES. BACKGROUND: MADDYZ/SHUTTERSTOCK, JOINTSTAR/SHUTTERSTOCK.

36 Antarctica IN A DAY

VIEWS | GLACIERS | ICE

Perhaps the greatest day trip in the world, travelers can fly from Cape Town to East Antarctica for a single day of adventures on the ice. While still expensive, these fly-in experiences remain the most affordable way to step onto the interior Antarctic continent without committing to a full expedition.

COURTESY OF WHITE DESERT

How to

Getting there and cost Fly in from Cape Town for the day and the cost runs from US$13,500–16,500.

Flightseeing Flights soar over the Antarctic ice sheet, which can be more than 3km thick in places.

Rocky oasis The Schirmacher Oasis, in Queen Maud Land, is reached by small aircraft and home to several inland camps. It's a narrow strip of land, 17km long and 3km wide, that remains ice free year-round, making it an 'oasis' in a landscape defined by ice.

COURTESY OF WHITE DESERT

COURTESY OF WHITE DESERT

Clockwise from bottom left Making glacier cocktails; Ice cave; Abseiling down a frozen cliff

Blue ice landscapes and exploration Ultima offers a short fly-in experience called 'The Ultima Day,' allowing travelers to visit interior Antarctica in about 24 hours. Guests depart Cape Town on an early-morning charter flight and fly to their blue ice runway in Queen Maud Land. After landing, they spend about 10 hours on the ice at Ultima's expedition camp, sharing a meal with polar crews and exploring nearby ice features, such as towering ice walls and the continental ice shelf, before flying back to South Africa the same day. For those wanting slightly longer on the continent, the company also offers an overnight option, a roughly 36-hour experience that includes a stay at their Oasis Camp.

Ice caves and glacier cocktails White Desert's 'Antarctica in a Day' experience offers a rare chance to visit the continent on a same-day return trip from Cape Town. Guests fly to their Wolf's Fang blue ice runway in Queen Maud Land, spending several hours exploring the Antarctic interior before returning to South Africa. Activities can include visiting glowing blue ice caves, abseiling down frozen cliffs and celebrating the moment at their ice bar with a cocktail served over ancient glacial ice. The tightly choreographed itinerary is designed to give travelers a short but immersive taste of Antarctica's landscapes and adventure in a single extraordinary day.

Other Day Trips

Besides these fly-in trips to the Antarctic interior, there are a few other ways to experience Antarctica in a single day. Charter flights from Punta Arenas sometimes offer day trips to King George Island in the South Shetland Islands with DAP (dapairline.com/en/antarctic-adventure), where visitors can briefly step ashore near research stations and penguin colonies before returning to Chile. There are also scenic sightseeing flights from Australia with Antarctic Flights (antarcticaflights.com) that fly over the Antarctic coastline and ice shelves without landing, giving passengers a rare aerial view of the continent before returning the same day.

■ By Sandie Kestell
Sandie is an Antarctica enthusiast. She traveled as a guest of Antarctic Logistics & Expeditions. Independent access to the South Pole is extraordinarily difficult and expensive. Lonely Planet retained full editorial control.

Journeys to the Pole

GETTING TO THE BOTTOM OF THE WORLD

It's been over 100 years since the Heroic Age of Antarctic Exploration and the race to the South Pole, and many people still feel drawn to the bottom of the world. For those lucky enough to visit the South Pole today, it's a very different journey.

HULTON ARCHIVE/GETTY IMAGES

Left Robert Falcon Scott's *Discovery* expedition **Centre** Roald Amundsen **Right** A member of Roald Amundsen's team with sled dogs

First Attempts

Robert Falcon Scott's *Discovery* expedition of 1901–04 was the first to attempt to reach the South Pole. The expedition had numerous scientific research goals, but the sledging journey to reach the South Pole was a key objective. Scott chose Ernest Shackleton as third officer, along with his close confidant Dr Edward Wilson, to make up his three-man team to attempt to reach the pole. Though they did use sledge-dogs to travel, and supporting parties of men joined them in the early stages of their journey to help with supplies, they made slow progress due to their lack of experience with dogs.

It soon became apparent that the food supplies for the men and the dogs were insufficient. All suffered greatly from undernourishment, not to mention frostbite, and as time went on, the men began showing symptoms of scurvy. The dogs were gradually killed to provide food for those who remained, but all were dead before long.

Before turning back, Scott and Wilson established a new farthest south record at 82° 17', having left Shackleton at a camp at 82° 15', too weak to continue south. Their return journey was a miserable grind for survival, manhauling the sledges in a desperately exhausted and starving state. Shackleton was so weak he was unable to pull the sledges anymore; after the party's arrival at their base camp, Scott sent him home to England rather than remain with the wintering party.

Shackleton later established a farthest south record of 88° 23' during his *Nimrod* expedition of 1907–09. Eager to return south after *Discovery*, Shackleton's four-man team relied on ponies rather than dogs but the ponies struggled

BAIN NEWS SERVICE, PUBLISHER/ WIKIMEDIA/PUBLIC DOMAIN

GRAPHIC HOUSE/ARCHIVE PHOTOS/GETTY IMAGES

with the conditions and surfaces and all perished on the trek, so the men were left to manhaul their sledges. They faced similar struggles to those Shackleton experienced on the earlier *Discovery* expedition: hunger, frostbite, exhaustion and the onset of scurvy. With fewer than 100 geographic miles left to the pole but alarmingly low food supplies, Shackleton decided that turning back was their only option for survival.

They suffered greatly, sinking into the deep snow as they slowly hauled supplies.

The Race to the Pole

The race to the pole between Scott and Roald Amundsen in the Antarctic summer of 1911–12 is the stuff of legend. The two expeditions could not have been more different. Amundsen, an expert in polar travel, relied on skis, dogs, and sledding and survival skills learned from the Inuit of the Canadian Arctic during his 1903–06 expedition to navigate the Northwest Passage. Scott, on the other hand, first became interested in Antarctic travel as a way to progress his career in the Navy. After his *Discovery* expedition, he was eager to return south and continue to make his mark. He favored ponies over dogs and pioneered the use of early motorized sledges. Scientific and geological research were of paramount importance to him. On the other hand, Amundsen's sole focus was reaching the pole and he was able to put all of his efforts into achieving this.

Neither expedition was expecting a race. Amundsen had initially planned to be the first to reach the North Pole, but after two claims for the North Pole were made by Frederick Cook, one of his shipmates on the *Belgica* expedition of 1897–99, and prolific Arctic explorer Robert Peary, Amundsen decided to

Five-Man Teams

Amundsen planned to bring five men to the pole: Helmer Hanssen, who had been a member of his Northwest Passage expedition; Sverre Hassel, a highly experienced dog driver; Oscar Wisting, a member of the Norwegian Navy; and expert skier Olav Bjaaland. Scott, on the other hand, organized his party in groups of four, only deciding when the final support party was turning back that he would take a fifth man to the pole: Edgar Evans. This meant reorganizing food and fuel rations. It was undoubtedly easier to manhaul sledges with an extra man, but it took longer to cook and melt snow for drinking water.

change his plans. Scott was already en route to Antarctica with his *Terra Nova* expedition when he learned Amundsen would be making an attempt on the pole. The South Pole was one of several objectives of the expedition, along with scientific research, survey and geological work.

Amundsen's five-man team set off from the Bay of Whales on an uncharted route and made excellent progress, though they did at times face major challenges with crevasses, and the process of killing some of their dogs along the way in order to boost food supplies took a serious mental toll on the men. The five-man polar party ultimately reached the South Pole on December 14, 1911 and made it safely back to their base camp and left Antarctica to share the news with the world before the end of January 1912. It was an extremely well-planned and well-executed expedition.

The men were severely run down, suffering from frostbite and having difficulty finding the supply depots they cached on the outbound journey.

To get to the pole, Scott relied on a combination of ponies, motor sledges and manhauling, with dogs in a support role. The motor sledges failed early on in the outbound journey. The dogs traveled further than planned but were turned back to be available to support the polar party on the final leg of their return journey. Like during Shackleton's previous attempt, the ponies performed poorly, being largely unsuitable for travel in Antarctic terrain. Their rations were inadequate and they suffered greatly, sinking into the deep snow as they slowly hauled supplies. Those that did not perish were shot for food. The men persevered, with support parties gradually returning to base, while the five-man polar party manhauled their sledges south. They finally arrived at the pole on January 17, 1912. It was a huge blow to find Amundsen's camp already there.

The party's return journey to their base at Cape Evans was disastrous. The men were severely run down, suffering from frostbite and having difficulty finding the supply depots they cached on the outbound journey. In addition, shortages of fuel at the depots, lower than expected temperatures for the time of year and the onset of scurvy created the conditions for disaster. Edgar Evans, the party's strongest man, was the first to perish, followed by Lawrence Oates. Scott, Wilson and Bowers carried on but blizzard conditions eventually confined them to their tent – just 11 miles (18km) from the next depot they desperately

HULTON-DEUTSCH COLLECTION/CORBIS/CORBIS VIA GETTY IMAGES

POPPERFOTO VIA GETTY IMAGES/GETTY IMAGES

POPPERFOTO VIA GETTY IMAGES/GETTY IMAGES

© CORBIS/CORBIS VIA GETTY IMAGES

needed to reach for food and fuel. It was 11 miles too far; the three men died in their tent. Their camp was discovered the following summer by members of their support party.

The Aviation Era

In the years following Amundsen and Scott's expeditions, attention soon turned to aviation. Richard E Byrd was the first to reach the pole by air in November 1929 in a return journey that took around 19 hours from the 'Little America' base on the Ross Ice Shelf. By way of comparison, it took Amundsen's party three months to get to the pole and back, while Scott's party had been underway for five months when the last of the group perished before reaching their base.

Flying has remained the dominant form of transport to reach the South Pole, though modern flights are a lot faster. Taking off from their base at Union Glacier in the Ellsworth Mountains, Antarctic Logistics & Expeditions (p183) flies travelers to the South Pole in a 1960s-era Basler DC-3 in around four hours. Gone are the hardships and lengthy time periods the early expeditions endured.

It is still possible to reach the pole in the style of the early explorers. Dogs have not been used on the continent since the 1990s, but ski expeditions that see adventurers pulling sledges and setting up their own field camps are a challenging possibility for those with the desire, stamina and funds that such an expedition requires. Modern clothing, equipment and communication tools have completely changed the game, as has our knowledge of the nutrition required for polar expeditions. Medical support and emergency services are still extremely limited, but in an emergency, satellite communication makes it possible for expedition parties to communicate with bases and operators.

Overnighting at the South Pole

If you are lucky enough to visit the South Pole as a tourist or expeditioner, there's only one place to stay: South Pole Camp operated by Antarctic Logistics & Expeditions. Located a few hundred meters from the Geographic South Pole, it is the southernmost resort in the world. Bright yellow two-person Arctic Oven tents – each named after a polar explorer – are neatly laid out in front of the dining tent where guests dine on the most southerly meal you could ever eat and raise a celebratory toast to those who struggled to reach the South Pole over a century ago.

From left to right Robert Falcon Scott; Robert Falcon Scott, Lawrence Oates, Edward Wilson and Edgar Evans at Roald Amundsen's camp; Edward Wilson with his pony; Richard E Byrd

Practicalities

Right Brown Bluff (p125), Antarctic Peninsula

GETTING THERE & PORTS OF DEPARTURE

Ushuaia, Argentina, is the main gateway to Antarctica. Expeditions also depart from Chile, South Africa, New Zealand and Australia. Some travelers fly to King George Island to board ships, while others fly directly to inland Antarctic camps, bypassing ships entirely.

GATEWAY PORTS

USHUAIA

Ushuaia (p34) is the main departure port for Antarctic voyages. Expedition ships dock at the central pier, and travelers are advised to arrive a day or two early in case of delays. Regular flights connect with Buenos Aires, and many companies arrange transfers and group hotels before departure.

ALTERNATIVES

Some voyages depart from Puerto Williams, Chile, while others occasionally start in Punta Arenas, Puerto Madryn, or Montevideo. A few itineraries begin in one port and end in another.

EXTENSIONS

Some trips include flights to the departure port, but independent travelers often opt out to spend extra time exploring Patagonia or Tierra del Fuego (p42) around Ushuaia or Punta Arenas.

FLIGHT TIMING Flights take about 2-2½ hours, and these trips are usually shorter than sail-only voyages because they skip the two-day Drake Passage crossing, averaging around eight days rather than the typical 10-20 days at sea. Some itineraries combine flying one way with sailing the Drake Passage the other, offering a balance between saving time and experiencing the full crossing.

FLY-CRUISE You can fly from Punta Arenas, Chile to King George Island (p97) in the South Shetland Islands, then board your expedition ship. This avoids the two-day sailing across the Drake Passage.

YACHT CHARTERS Some yacht charters also operate from King George Island, and a small number of voyages begin or end in Stanley in the Falkland Islands, which is usually reached by LATAM flights via Punta Arenas.

FLIGHTS & WEATHER

Flights depend heavily on visibility and conditions at King George Island (pictured below), where cloud, wind and low visibility can quickly close the runway.

Delays and cancelations are common, sometimes lasting several days, and in some cases, entire trips are canceled if conditions don't improve.

If flights cannot operate for several days, ships may sail across the Drake Passage to collect or drop off passengers instead.

GOLDILOCK PROJECT/SHUTTERSTOCK

SOUTHERN ROUTES

New Zealand Voyages by ship to the Ross Sea in Antarctica usually depart from Dunedin or Invercargill (Bluff) in New Zealand, with occasional departures from Christchurch (Timaru). Operators also arrange transfers from larger hubs like Queenstown, a major South Island travel gateway, helping travelers connect.

Australia Some sea voyages depart from Hobart in Tasmania, Australia. Occasionally, expeditions begin in Australia or New Zealand, sail to Antarctica, and complete a semi-circumnavigation of the continent before finishing in Ushuaia, typically taking around 30–35 days.

Interior Flights Trips to Antarctica's interior generally depart from Cape Town, South Africa, or Punta Arenas, Chile, flying to remote base camps operated by ALE (Antarctic Logistics & Expeditions; pictured below at Union Glacier, p195), White Desert or Ultima Antarctica Expeditions in Queen Maud Land. Flights typically take five to six hours and depend on weather and visibility.

STEPHANIE JACKSON/ALAMY

LIMITATIONS OF FLYOVERS

There are limits to what you can see on an overflight. Individual buildings may be visible if you are flying over research stations, but animals are impossible to spot, even with binoculars. Passengers move around the cabin for views, and the cheapest tickets usually do not guarantee window access. Even with window seats, views are often shared or rotated during the flight, so expect to swap partway through for a fair chance to see the landscape.

HOW MUCH FOR...

Antarctic Peninsula cruise **from US$8,000**

Fly-cruise Antarctica trip **from US$12,000**

Ross Sea expedition cruise **from US$30,000**

Interior Antarctica fly-in camp **from US$40,000**

CHOOSING WHERE TO GO

Antarctic expeditions visit several different regions, each offering distinct landscapes, wildlife and travel experiences. The Antarctic Peninsula is the most commonly visited area, but itineraries may also include South Georgia and the Falkland Islands. Others go to the Ross Sea or fly into interior and East Antarctica.

ANTARCTIC PENINSULA

Route & Duration
Most Antarctic cruises visit the Antarctic Peninsula and depart from Ushuaia, Argentina. Crossing the Drake Passage takes about two days each way, accounting for four days of the itinerary. The shortest sailing trips are usually around 10 days.

Yachts
Sailing voyages by yacht tend to be longer because of slower travel speeds and flexible itineraries with more operational days. Crossing the Drake can take 3–6 days depending on speeds and weather.

LOUIELEA/SHUTTERSTOCK

ANTARCTIC PENINSULA TIPS When comparing trips, look closely at the number of operational days in Antarctica rather than just the total trip length.

Once embarkation and disembarkation days are included, the shortest trips may only have about four operational days in Antarctica.

Landings depend heavily on conditions, and strong weather in the Drake can occasionally shorten itineraries.

ANTARCTIC CIRCLE & WEDDELL SEA

Route & Duration Longer Peninsula voyages continue south of 66° 33' S to cross the Antarctic Circle. These trips usually last 12–14 days and typically include at least six operational days on the Peninsula.

Reaching the Antarctic Circle requires sailing further south; these itineraries are longer than standard Peninsula voyages.

Weddell Sea Some itineraries also attempt to enter the Weddell Sea, conditions permitting, alongside visits to the Peninsula. Sea ice plays a major role in determining how far ships can travel south along the west side of the Peninsula and into the Weddell Sea.

Snow Hill Island A small number of specialized Weddell Sea voyages attempt to visit the emperor penguin colony near Snow Hill, though access depends heavily on sea ice. When possible, helicopters transport passengers from the ship across the ice to a landing site near the colony.

SOUTH GEORGIA & THE FALKLAND ISLANDS

Extended Voyages The longest itineraries combine Antarctica with the Falkland Islands (Islas Malvinas) and South Georgia. These voyages typically last about three weeks, though some may be slightly shorter.

Sailing Distances Long crossings are required between the Falklands, South Georgia and the Antarctic Peninsula. Sailing between these destinations can take around 2–3 days each way.

Operational Days Because of these long passages, it is important to check how many landing days are scheduled in each location. Often itineraries have two days in the Falkland Islands and four days in South Georgia.

ROSS SEA & SUBANTARCTIC ISLANDS

Duration Voyages to the Ross Sea explore one of the most isolated parts of Antarctica. These trips usually last around a month due to the long sailing distances involved.

Season & Planning The Ross Sea season is short, generally limited to January and February when the sea ice opens enough for ships to access the region. Review itineraries to clarify how many landing opportunities and island stops are planned.

Subantarctic Islands Many itineraries include visits to remote islands along the route, which vary between voyages depending on permits and operator itineraries. Stops are usually set in advance, though landings may be canceled or adjusted at short notice if weather or sea conditions prevent safe access.

DESTINATION	TYPICAL TRIP LENGTH
Antarctic Peninula	10+ days
Antarctic Circle & Weddell Sea	12–14 days
South Georgia & the Falkland Islands	3 weeks
Ross Sea & Subantarctic	1 month

SANDIE KESTELL/LONELY PLANET

EAST ANTARCTICA FLY-IN TRIPS

Unlike cruise-based expeditions, trips to East Antarctica or the South Pole involve flying directly to the continent. Most itineraries last around a week, though some may be longer depending on activities and weather.

Visitors stay at small inland camps (South Pole Camp pictured above, p209) that can vary from insulated tents, small cabins to luxury pods. Shared lounges and dining areas host meals and briefings. Most camps have heated bathrooms and showers, while some offer private ensuites, lounges, spas or saunas.

CHOOSING TRANSPORT & CABINS

Modern Antarctic expedition ships vary widely in size, comfort and price. While early tourist voyages often used converted research vessels with shared facilities, today's fleet ranges from small expedition ships focused on landings to large luxury vessels offering extensive onboard amenities.

SHIP SIZE & PASSENGER NUMBERS

Passenger limits Ship size impacts time spent ashore. IAATO (p227) guidelines allow only 100 passengers ashore at one time at most landing sites, with some locations limiting visits to 50 people at a time.

Small ships (under 100 passengers) All passengers can usually land at the same time, giving you more time ashore. Smaller ships are also more likely to visit landing sites with stricter limits.

Medium ships (100–200 passengers) These vessels typically run split operations, where half the passengers go ashore while the other half take a Zodiac cruise, then the groups switch. Most operators aim to offer two landings or excursions per day.

Large expedition ships (200–500 passengers) These ships often run one landing period per day, rotating groups through the site. Time ashore is limited.

Very large ships (over 500 passengers) Ships carrying more than 500 passengers cannot make landings in Antarctica, meaning the continent is viewed from the ship only.

GRAFISSIMO/GETTY IMAGES

YACHTS & TALL SHIPS

Small vessels A small but growing number of travelers reach Antarctica aboard sailing yachts or expedition sailboats.

Passenger limits Most IAATO-registered yachts carry 12 passengers or fewer, allowing them to land without the same restrictions as larger ships. Several dozen operate in Antarctic waters each season and must follow the same environmental guidelines.

Tall ships Larger sailing vessels also visit Antarctica. One of the best known is Bark EUROPA, a three-masted barque carrying fewer than 42 passengers, where guests can help hoist sails, stand watch and climb the rigging.

CABIN TYPES & LAYOUT

Shared cabins The most budget-friendly option is a triple or quad shared cabin, where solo travelers may be paired with same-gender roommates unless they pay a single supplement.

Standard cabins The most common accommodation is a twin cabin, with beds that can usually be configured as either two singles or one double.

Single cabins Some ships offer single occupancy cabins, though availability is usually limited and they tend to sell out quickly.

Suites Higher-category cabins include larger suites, with the most premium option often the owner's or captain's suite. Some luxury ships include butler service.

Bathrooms Modern expedition ships almost always have ensuite bathrooms, and shared bathrooms are now uncommon.

Cabin views Lower deck cabins often have portholes (which are sometimes closed in rough seas), while higher deck cabins may have larger windows. Many newer ships also feature private balconies.

Motion There's an industry saying that 'the more you pay, the more you sway.' Cabins on higher decks or toward the bow of the ship tend to experience more movement, which may matter if you are prone to seasickness.

FLY-IN CAMPS

Setting Fly-in camps in interior Antarctica are small, accommodating only a dozen or so guests at a time. Aside from Union Glacier Camp (p195), the other camps offer luxury accommodation, though the level of amenities varies.

Accommodations Camps provide heated sleeping quarters such as insulated tents, pods or small cabins designed for polar conditions.

Facilities Shared lounges and dining areas serve as gathering spaces for meals, briefings and social time. Most camps also have heated bathroom facilities and showers.

Services Meals are prepared by in-house chefs and served communally.

Comfort Most camps include higher-end amenities such as private ensuite bathrooms, saunas or spas, and curated dining experiences.

Operators The three operators are White Desert, ALE (Antarctic Logistics & Expeditions) and Ultima. White Desert runs luxury camps in Queen Maud Land, Ultima operates Oasis Camp in the Schirmacher Oasis, and ALE runs Union Glacier Camp and Three Glaciers Retreat for expeditions and South Pole trips.

COSTS & MONEY

Antarctica isn't cheap. It's remote, and operating tours there is expensive. But price is only one factor in choosing a trip. Sometimes a small increase in what you pay will get you a much more in-depth experience, which is important for what may be a once-in-a-lifetime journey.

SHORT TRIP COSTS

Fly-in day trip to East Antarctica **from US$13,500**

Short multi-day fly-in trip to interior Antarctica **from US$25,000**

Fly-cruise trip without Drake Passage **from US$13,500**

HOLGER LEUE/GETTY IMAGES

BUDGETING YOUR TRIP

Most Antarctic expedition cruises fall have a midrange price tag (see box on right).

Adventure activities such as kayaking (pictured above), diving, camping, or mountaineering are often optional add-ons. They are not included in the base fare of many Antarctic expeditions. Add-on activities should be booked far in advance as they sell out quickly. Occasionally, spaces become available on board.

LAST MINUTE VS BOOKING AHEAD

In the past, travelers could sometimes find last-minute discounted berths in Ushuaia just days before departure, but these deals are far less common today as voyages frequently sell out earlier. However, with many operators competing on Peninsula routes, discounts and promotional sales are common online, particularly for travelers who book well in advance.

NANCY PAUWELS/SHUTTERSTOCK

DISCOUNTS

Sign up for operator mailing lists and follow expedition companies on social media, where last-minute deals and early-bird offers are often shared. Specialist polar travel agents and blogs also highlight discounts, especially for shoulder-season departures or unsold cabins released closer to departure.

NANCY PAUWELS/SHUTTERSTOCK

BUDGET

Less than US$13,000

- Antarctic Peninsula cruises start around US$6000–8000 for 9–11 day voyages, typically in triple-share cabins or lower-category twin rooms.
- Scenic Antarctic fly-over flights from Australia start at about AU$1200 and can reach AU$8000 depending on seating.

MIDRANGE

US$13,000–$40,000

- 10–14-day Antarctic Peninsula voyages typically start around US$12,000–16,000, depending on ship and cabin type.
- 18–22-day voyages that include the Falkland Islands and South Georgia usually start at US$15,000–20,000.
- Ross Sea expeditions start around US$30,000 due to their length and remoteness.
- Some short multi-day fly-in trips to interior Antarctica begin around US$25,000.

TOP END

More than US$40,000

- Luxury expedition cruises with balcony suites or premium ships often exceed US$40,000 per person.
- Most fly-in expeditions to camps in East Antarctica cost between US$70,000–80,000.
- Extreme expeditions such as climbing Vinson Massif cost about US$58,000, while skiing to the South Pole can cost around US$85,000.
- Specialist fly-in trips that include a visit to the South Pole typically start around US$67,000 and can exceed US$100,000.

ADD-ON ACTIVITIES

Kayaking One of the most common add-ons on expedition ships, usually offered as a multi-day program with small guided groups. Ranges from US$600–1000.

Stand-up paddleboarding (SUP) Short guided paddles near landing sites in calm conditions. Offered on a limited number of ships and can cost US$200–400.

Snorkeling Guided excursions in drysuits with specialized equipment can run between US$200–400 per outing.

Scuba diving Cold-water dives for certified divers with specialized guides and equipment. Cost US$800–1500.

Camping Overnight experience sleeping on the snow in a bivy bag or swag (a compact, all-in-one sleeping tent). Usually offered once per voyage if conditions allow early in the season and run around US$250–400.

Snowshoeing Guided hikes using snowshoes when snow cover is sufficient. Cost US$100–300.

Mountaineering Guided climbing or glacier trekking on select voyages can cost US$300–800.

Ski touring Offered on some early-season departures when snow conditions allow. Runs around US$500–1200.

Photography workshops Small-group instruction with professional photographers as a program throughout the trip. Can cost US$300–900.

Helicopter excursions Scenic flights or landings on remote locations offered on ships equipped with helicopters. Can cost US$200–1000+ per flight, depending on duration.

Submarine dives Deep-water submersible dives are offered on a few luxury vessels, such as those operated by Viking or Scenic. Can cost US$500–1000+ per dive.

LIFE ONBOARD

Polar voyages operate differently from typical cruises, and it's common to feel tired during sea days. Days are filled with lectures, briefings and activities. Schedules are posted daily; on shore days, passengers usually go out twice, with landings or Zodiac cruises, ending with an evening recap and briefing.

ONBOARD FACILITIES

Spaces Expedition ships usually include dining rooms, lounges for relaxing between excursions, lecture halls for daily briefings, small libraries with polar books, and observation decks for wildlife watching.

Services Laundry service and a small medical clinic are standard on most vessels.

Wellness Many ships also include a gym, sauna or small spa, and some have a wellness instructor who offers classes such as yoga, stretching or meditation.

Luxury ships Higher-end expedition vessels may offer multiple restaurants, larger spas, outdoor hot tubs or pools, and panoramic observation lounges.

Drinks Some ships include house wine, beer and soft drinks with meals, while others charge separately for alcoholic beverages.

HOLGER LEUE/GETTY IMAGES

SHIP SAFETY IN ROUGH SEAS

Stability Keep one hand free for the ship, using railings or supports if the vessel rolls suddenly. Take care on stairs, ladders and corridors where sudden movement could lead to falls or injuries.

Obstacles Watch for raised door sills, fittings and other ship hardware. The outer decks can be slippery when wet, snowy, icy or oiled, so move cautiously. Ship doors are heavy and can swing quickly, so keep fingers clear of door frames.

Cabins Store loose items in your cabin when rough seas are expected. Placing a wet napkin under a drink can help keep it from sliding across the table during rough seas.

THE DRAKE PASSAGE & OTHER CROSSINGS

Route More than 90% of Antarctic Peninsula cruises depart from Ushuaia, Argentina, crossing the Drake Passage, a roughly 1000km stretch of open ocean between South America and Antarctica.

Conditions With no landmasses to block weather systems, strong westerly winds and storms frequently move through the area. Waves average 3–5m during a standard Drake Passage crossing.

Other crossings Similar sea conditions are encountered when sailing between Antarctica, South Georgia and the Falkland Islands, as well as in the Ross Sea between the Antarctic continent and the subantarctic islands.

Navigation Modern expedition ships monitor weather closely and may adjust routes to avoid large storms. Once ships reach sheltered coastal waters, the motion usually decreases significantly.

H. MARK WEIDMAN PHOTOGRAPHY/ALAMY

ONBOARD SCIENCE

Many Antarctic expedition ships host scientists who collect data and conduct fieldwork across the Southern Ocean. Groups like Oceanites (oceanites.org) monitor penguins and seabirds, while others study whales, plankton, ocean conditions, bird flu and climate change. Scientists gather observations across wide areas and often lecture on board, sharing insights with travelers.

ON SHORE & INLAND

Navigating the Antarctic requires embracing flexibility, as shifting environmental conditions and strict safety protocols constantly reshape daily expedition itineraries.

WEATHER & CHANGING PLANS

Conditions Antarctic itineraries are dictated by wind, waves and sea ice, and plans often change accordingly.

Flexibility Expedition teams typically prepare multiple backup plans to adapt to changing conditions.

Landings Specific sites such as Port Lockroy or the Lemaire Channel may be planned, but no landings are guaranteed. Ships reserve landing slots through IAATO (p227) to ensure only one vessel visits a site at a time.

Exceptions Grytviken is one of the more reliable stops, as ships must clear customs and undergo biosecurity checks there when visiting South Georgia.

Weather impacts Strong winds, large waves, sea ice, icebergs or brash ice can cancel or shorten landings, sometimes turning them into Zodiac cruises instead.

Katabatic winds In places like South Georgia, sudden katabatic winds can rush down from glaciers and mountains, producing powerful gusts that can quickly change conditions.

Interior weather Differs from ship travel, with operations built around chasing safe windows. Because trips focus on reaching the South Pole or emperor penguin colonies, operators constantly monitor conditions and adjust flights, routes and schedules at a moment's notice.

ON-SHORE CONSIDERATIONS

Boundaries Expedition teams mark landing areas with flags to show where visitors can and cannot walk.

Wildlife Flags may mark the edges of penguin colonies or sensitive areas such as crevassed terrain. Wildlife calls the shots, and visitors must give animals space in accordance with IAATO protocols.

Paths Penguins often create well-worn routes known as penguin highways, which visitors are asked to avoid using.

Seals In places like South Georgia, fur seals can be aggressive. Standing your ground and appearing larger usually discourages a charge.

Briefings Each landing begins with a short briefing explaining the site, what to see, and the return time to the ship.

Guides Expedition staff are positioned around the landing area to help, answer questions and share information about wildlife, history, and the landscape.

Toilets There are no bathroom facilities on Peninsula landings.

LIZ CARLSON

ZODIACS

Zodiacs are the backbone of Antarctic expedition travel. These small inflatable boats are used for most landings and shoreline exploration, reaching places larger vessels cannot. Used for both landings and wildlife cruising, they play a central role in daily operations and close-up experiences.

Capacity They usually carry 9–16 passengers plus a driver.

Design Their shallow draft allows them to maneuver among icebergs and reach beaches ships cannot access.

Stability Multiple air-filled compartments keep the boats afloat even if sections are punctured.

Boarding Getting in and out is usually straightforward in calm weather, but can be more difficult in swell or waves.

Lifejackets Passengers must wear a properly fitted life jacket that does not interfere with the inflation mechanism.

Equipment Avoid carrying excessive weight, such as multiple cameras attached to belts.

Clothing Waterproof outerwear and a waterproof bag are essential because of spray and waves.

Movement Always check with the driver before standing or kneeling, and follow crew instructions when boarding, landing and during the ride.

ACTIVITIES

Some ships offer optional paid activities instead of regular excursions, including kayaking, paddleboarding, snorkeling, diving and photography programs, with seasonal options like skiing, mountaineering, snowshoeing or camping. Spaces are limited and book quickly. At fly-in camps, most activities are included and organized around weather, with options like glacier trekking, skiing, mountaineering, fat biking and scenic flights.

KAYAKING & CAMPING PRACTICALITIES

Operators typically provide equipment for add-on excursions (p219), such as drysuits for kayaking. Another common add-on is camping, where participants sleep in single-person bivy bags rather than tents. Biosecurity rules ensure camping locations are at a distance from wildlife, and temporary toilet areas are dug into the snow and removed afterward.

HEALTH & SAFETY

Travel to Antarctica involves remote conditions where medical support and emergency services are extremely limited. Accidents and injuries here can have higher consequences because of the remoteness. Expedition ships carry trained staff and basic facilities, but travelers should understand the risks and arrive well prepared.

MOBILITY & PHYSICAL REQUIREMENTS

Good mobility Important on Antarctic expeditions. Passengers must move around the ship independently, use stairs and complete safety procedures without assistance. Elevators may exist but can close in rough seas, and rolling conditions require travelers to be steady on their feet. More demanding expeditions, such as sailing voyages or skiing to the South Pole, require higher levels of fitness.

Landings Most excursions involve stepping into and out of Zodiacs from a moving ship and walking across wet beaches, snow or uneven ground. Expedition teams provide guidance, but guests must maneuver safely on their own, and may remain onboard if conditions are difficult.

Limited emergency response IAATO states that Antarctica is severe, changeable and potentially dangerous, and visitors should not expect a rescue service in the way they might elsewhere.

MEDICAL CARE

Antarctica has no hospitals, pharmacies or doctors offices. Expedition ships carry a small infirmary with a doctor, basic supplies and sometimes additional medical staff. Serious emergencies may require evacuation to another country, which can be delayed by weather or distance, and could end a voyage early. Bring sufficient medications and personal supplies. Some operators require medical clearance before travel.

Shipboard Safety
Maritime law requires every vessel to conduct a lifeboat drill and participation is mandatory. Additional safety drills may take place during the voyage, sometimes while passengers are ashore, but passengers are always informed in advance.

ANDREW PEACOCK/GETTY IMAGES

BDPHOTO/GETTY IMAGES

OTHER AILMENTS

Dryness Antarctica's extremely dry environment can lead to dehydration. Some travelers bring small travel humidifiers.

Altitude Visitors to inland areas such as the South Pole or East Antarctica may experience mild altitude sickness.

Cold Frostbite and hypothermia are rare among tourists, but dress in layers, wear a hat, stay dry and change wet clothing.

Sunburn and snow blindness Even on cloudy days, use sunscreen and UV-filtering sunglasses or goggles.

Illness Viruses can spread quickly on ships. Wash your hands and wear a mask if unwell.

Health limits Activities like polar plunges (pictured above) aren't advised for travelers with medical conditions like heart issues.

Strong odours Wildlife colonies can be pungent, with guano and carrion smells that shift with the wind.

ACCESSIBLE TRAVEL

Operators Accessibility varies widely between operators, ships and itineraries, so check details before booking.

Ship access Some ships offer accessible cabins and lifts, but layouts differ and access may be limited.

Support Crew cannot provide personal care, so travelers needing assistance must bring a companion.

Medical Onboard facilities are basic, and access to medication or treatment is limited.

Evacuation Medical evacuation is complex, often requiring flights to South America and favorable conditions.

Alternatives Overflights or ship-based trips without landings may be more accessible options.

SEASICKNESS

Seasickness is common in the Southern Ocean, especially during crossings like the Drake Passage. Modern expedition ships often have stabilizers to reduce motion, and expedition leaders usually warn passengers when rough seas are expected.

Prevention Spend time outside the cabin, keep a view of the horizon and eat lightly. Choosing midship lower-deck cabins can help reduce symptoms and accustom you to the motion.

Medication Motion sickness medicines such as dimenhydrinate, meclizine, promethazine or scopolamine patches are commonly used and should be taken before symptoms begin. Some travelers also rely on ginger or acupressure wristbands.

POSITIVE-IMPACT TRAVEL

Tips to leave a lighter footprint and have a positive impact on local communities.

ON YOUR TRIP

Protection Antarctica is protected under the Antarctic Treaty system, which sets clear environmental rules for visitors. Tens of thousands of people visit the Antarctic Peninsula each year, and many land at the same sites, making responsible behavior essential.

Regulations Violating environmental guidelines can trigger penalties under your home country's Antarctic legislation, including fines or other legal consequences. Passengers who ignore wildlife distances or site rules may be removed from landings or barred from further excursions.

Operators Responsible travelers should choose companies that follow strict environmental standards. Most reputable operators are members of IAATO, which sets guidelines for visitor limits, wildlife protection and safe ship operations.

Practices Look for operators that emphasize environmental briefings, strong biosecurity procedures, and partnerships with scientific research or conservation programs. Operators that emphasize science lectures, citizen science and conservation education help visitors better understand and protect the region.

BIOSPHOTO/ALAMY

LEAVE A SMALL FOOTPRINT

Ships Modern vessels are built with fuel-efficient engines, hull designs and stabilizers to reduce emissions. Some vessels reuse engine heat to warm cabins or water, to reduce the energy demands onboard. Antarctic vessels must use marine gas oil or other low-sulfur fuels, since heavy fuel oil is banned in Antarctic waters.

Fly-in Camps are fully removable with no permanent structures. Visitor numbers are kept low to reduce disturbance and environmental impact. Camps use solar panels (pictured above) and heating to limit fuel use, and all waste is removed from Antarctica for recycling or disposal under Antarctic Treaty requirements.

REDUCING EMISSIONS

Sustainability certifications Some operators offer carbon offset programs or maintain certifications such as B Corp (bcorporation.net).

Carbon-neutral options White Desert's fly-in camps operate as carbon-neutral facilities.

Aviation emissions White Desert was the first Antarctic tourism operator to trial sustainable aviation fuel, which can cut aviation emissions by up to 80%.

JORDANLYE/GETTY IMAGES

WILDLIFE DISEASES & AVIAN FLU

Wildlife in the subantarctic and Antarctica have experienced disease outbreaks, including avian cholera and highly pathogenic avian influenza (HPAI or bird flu). Avian flu has caused major seabird and marine mammal die-offs. It reached South Georgia in 2023 and the Peninsula in 2024. Scientists and operators monitor impacts closely, with strict protocols in place to ensure the health and safety of guests and to prevent the spread of diseases between wildlife colonies. Expect sporadic outbreaks, and follow current IAATO guidance.

IAATO

Most expedition cruise companies are members of the International Association of Antarctica Tour Operators (IAATO; iaato.org).

Founded in 1991, IAATO promotes safe, environmentally responsible travel. It sets standards for tourism, including wildlife distances, landing limits and biosecurity measures.

IAATO works with governments under the Antarctic Treaty System to develop guidelines for visitor behavior, wildlife protection, landing procedures and ship operations.

STRICT CHECKS

Biosecurity checks take place before excursions begin, and some items may not pass inspection and must stay onboard. These can include beanies with pom-poms, Velcro, or backpack mesh and straps that can catch debris.

BIOSECURITY

Strict biosecurity rules prevent the introduction of non-native species, seeds or microbes into Antarctica's fragile ecosystems. Required under the Antarctic Treaty and enforced by IAATO operators, similar protocols apply across regions including the Ross Sea, East Antarctica and many uninhabited subantarctic islands.

Cleaning Before going ashore, passengers attend briefings and clean outer gear. Expedition staff check boots, Velcro, pockets and bags for seeds, soil or organic material. This process is repeated before visiting places such as South Georgia and the Falklands.

Preparation Travelers can prepare in advance by cleaning gear at home. Fleece and backpack straps often trap seeds and debris.

Disinfection Boots, hiking poles and tripods are disinfected in a Virkon foot bath before and after landings.

Precautions Visitors are asked not to sit or place items on the ground, keep distance from wildlife, and ensure clothing is clean and free of debris or guano.

ESSENTIAL NUTS & BOLTS

SHIP TIME

Timekeeping in Antarctica is flexible, and expedition ships usually stay on the time zone of their departure port, often Argentina time (UTC–3). Ships may adjust time zones at their discretion.

CAMP TIME

White Desert and Ultima operate on Cape Town time (UTC+2), and ALE's Union Glacier Camp runs on Chilean time (UTC–3).

SUBANTARCTIC TIME

Macquarie Island uses Tasmania time (UTC+10 or UTC+11), the New Zealand Subantarctic Islands follow New Zealand time (UTC+12 or UTC+13) and South Georgia uses UTC–2. The Falkland Islands (Islas Malvinas) use UTC-3.

INSURANCE FOR ANTARCTIC TRAVEL

Ship voyages Standard Antarctic Peninsula cruises typically require around US$100,000–200,000 in evacuation coverage, though many operators recommend US$250,000–500,000.

Fly-in expeditions Trips to inland Antarctica or the South Pole usually require higher evacuation coverage, often US$300,000–500,000 or more, because evacuations from interior camps are more complex.

Activities Travelers participating in activities such as kayaking, mountaineering, skiing or diving should ensure these are covered.

POWER, CHARGING & CONNECTIVITY

Internet coverage There is no mobile reception in Antarctica, and signal is lost soon after leaving Ushuaia. Small vessels may have limited or no internet. Camps rely on satellite internet, usually in communal areas.

Internet on ships Many expedition ships offer Starlink satellite internet, though access may be limited or cost extra.

Power Ships usually have reliable power, but access can be limited in remote camps, so bring a portable battery pack, especially for essential or medical devices.

Charging devices on ships Expedition vessels usually provide 110–240V outlets, depending on the ship. Many newer ships include universal outlets and USB ports in cabins for charging.

Charging devices in camps Fly-in camps generate electricity on site using generators and sometimes solar power. Devices can usually be charged in cabins or communal lounge areas at camps. Because power is generated locally in remote camps, guests are encouraged to be mindful of electricity use when charging devices.

ICE CLASS RATING
Most ships visiting Antarctica are ice-strengthened expedition vessels. For most voyages, standard ice-class ships are sufficient.

FAMILY TRAVEL
Many operators have minimum age limits (often 8–12), and itineraries may not be suited to younger children.

NOISE
Cabins near engines, anchors or public spaces can be noisy, especially during maneuvers or early-morning arrivals.

CURRENCY & TIPPING
US dollars are standard on most ships and camps, though some places accept multiple currencies.

Many operators use an onboard account system, with purchases settled at the end. Credit cards are usually required.

The British pound is used in some territories, including the Falklands.

Tipping is customary at the end of the trip, with most operators suggesting about US$15–25 per person per day for the crew onboard. Some operators also allow separate tipping collectively for the expedition team.

DRONES Recreational drone use in Antarctica is prohibited under IAATO and Antarctic Treaty guidelines to protect wildlife and ensure safety. Drone operations are limited to permitted professionals or researchers, with strict rules on altitude, wildlife distance and avoiding stations or protected areas.

AURORA AUSTRALIS Chances of seeing the aurora australis (Southern Lights) from an expedition ship are low. During tourism season, austral summer (December to February), long daylight hours limit darkness. There is a small chance in March, but most Peninsula voyages lack the latitude and sufficiently dark night hours for reliable viewing.

SAMOILA IONUT/SHUTTERSTOCK

RESOURCES

International Association of Antarctica Tour Operators (IAATO; iaato.org)

Antarctic Treaty Secretariat (ats.aq)

Commission for the Conservation of Antarctic Marine Living Resources (CCAMLR; ccamlr.org)

Scientific Committee on Antarctic Research (SCAR; scar.org)

Australian Antarctic Division (antarctica.gov.au)

New Zealand Department of Conservation (DOC; doc.govt.nz)

The UK Antarctic Heritage Trust (UKAHT; ukaht.org)

Antarctic Heritage Trust (nzaht.org)

South Georgia Heritage Trust (sght.org)

Latest information from World Organization of Animal Health (woah.org/en/disease/avian-influenza)

Packing
LIST

Layering up or down will allow you to adapt to changing conditions.

01 Base layers
Lightweight underwear, socks and sports bra followed by a long-sleeved top and full-length bottom layer, ideally all made from merino wool.

02 Mid layers
A thin fleece or heavyweight top and bottom, along with heavyweight woolen socks.

03 Insulation layer
A thick fleece, or a down or synthetic insulated jacket.

04 Sunscreen
Use sunscreen and lip balm with SPF 50 even if it's overcast.

05 Outer layer
Waterproof and windproof trousers and jacket with a hood to keep you warm and dry in the wind and snow.

06 Gloves & mittens
Layer your gloves to keep your hands warm. We recommend a thin liner glove under a midweight waterproof outer mitten.

07 Goggles
A cozier option in snowy or extremely cold

01 DMITRY NAUMOV/SHUTTERSTOCK, JIANG ZHONGYAN/SHUTTERSTOCK, SUPREEYA.CH/SHUTTERSTOCK, BEGUN1983/SHUTTERSTOCK, VLADIRI/SHUTTERSTOCK, **02** ISLAM STOCK PHOTO SELLER/SHUTTERSTOCK, SANKAI/GETTY IMAGES, VALKOINEN/SHUTTERSTOCK, **03** LILKIN/SHUTTERSTOCK, **04** CEMBER TECH/SHUTTERSTOCK, TALE/SHUTTERSTOCK, **05** TARZHANOVA/SHUTTERSTOCK, LANDSCAPEMANIA/SHUTTERSTOCK, **06** HEKLA/SHUTTERSTOCK, NAKPHOTOS/GETTY IMAGES, **07** GJOROVSKI GORAN/

conditions. Look for 100% UV protection.

08 Sunglasses
Look for 100% UV protection with side coverage for maximum protection.

09 Daypack & dry bag
To carry your camera, extra layers, binoculars and more on excursions. A dry bag is useful for Zodiac excursions.

10 Expedition jacket
Most operators provide an insulated parka as your outermost layer.

11 Headwear
Wear a wool or fleece hat or beanie that covers your ears. It should fit snugly so that the wind does not blow it off your head.

12 Swimwear
For the polar plunge.

13 Buff or neck gaiter
Protect your neck from the elements and use it for partial face protection.

14 Footwear
Heavy winter hiking boots. Your operator may also provide or rent knee-high waterproof boots.

SHUTTERSTOCK, **08** FORDHAM DABNEY/SHUTTERSTOCK, **09** OLGAUA/SHUTTERSTOCK, FRANTICOO/SHUTTERSTOCK, **10** DANIIL DUBOV/GETTY IMAGES, **11** SAMINAMUNEER1/SHUTTERSTOCK, **12** MAGDALENA WIELOBOB/SHUTTERSTOCK, OLGAGI/SHUTTERSTOCK, **13** OLGAGI/SHUTTERSTOCK, **14** NANISIMOVA/SHUTTERSTOCK

Index

000 Map pages

C

D

E

000 Map pages

S

000 Map pages

'That time I visited Macquarie Island and was surrounded by penguins and seals, I couldn't believe the scale of the wildlife.'

LIZ CARLSON

LIZ CARLSON, SASHA_GERASIMOV/SHUTTERSTOCK

'When humpback whales breached in every direction as we sailed through Patagonia Bay, and a family of them dove alongside the ship.'

ALEXIS AVERBUCK

THIS BOOK

This 1st edition of Lonely Planet's *Experience Antarctica* guidebook was researched and written by Alexis Averbuck and Liz Carlson, with contributions by Brekke Fletcher and Sandie Kestell. This guidebook was produced by the following:

Destination Editor Alicia Johnson

Coordinating Editor Anita Isalska

Production Editor Robin Yule

Cartographer Anthony Phelan

Image Researcher Ania Lenihan

Assisting Editor Kevin Ebbutt

Cover researcher Katelyn Perry

Thanks Sasha Drew, Jenna Myers, Darren O'Connell, Vicky Smith, Saralinda Turner

Travel to Antarctica is logistically complex and costly. To make on-the-ground research possible, we may collaborate with reputable expedition operators who provide logistical support such as transport and accommodations. These arrangements do not influence our editorial decisions. All recommendations are based on independent assessment and reflect our authors' honest experiences. We do not accept payment in exchange for coverage, and inclusion in this guide is never guaranteed.